MATTERS
OF THE
HEART

While the author has made every attempt to provide accurate telephone numbers, internet addresses or other resource information at the time of publication, the author assumes no responsibility for errors or changes that occur after publication.

The names and characterizations in this book are drawn from the author's friends, surveys and personal experiences. In order to maintain their anonymity, some identifying characteristics and details have been changed.

This book is not intended as a substitute for the medical advice of physicians. The reader should regularly consult a physician in matters relating to anyone's health and particularly with respect to any symptoms that may require diagnosis or medical attention.

Cover and book design by Phipps Advertising LLC

Editing by John Peragine

Scripture quotations marked (NIV) are taken from the Holy Bible: New International Version NIV® ©1973, 1978, 1894 International Bible Society.

ISBN-13: 978-1537003931

ISBN-10: 1537003933

The book is lovingly dedicated
to my parents,
Floyd and Beth Gunn,

and all my friends' parents as well.

TABLE OF CONTENTS

APPENDIX

Foreword

I am honored that Susan asked me to participate in her book in this way. I remember the Gunn family with great affection. My son attended the junior high school that bears his name, Floyd M. Gunn Junior High School. I had the good fortune of being one of both Floyd and Beth Gunn's personal physicians. They lived a good long fruitful life and were quite elderly when they passed. They are missed by many.

There are few people better suited to writing a book on caregiving than Susan, who participated in every aspect of her parents' medical care and medical decisions. She was present on all their office visits and most days when they were hospitalized. Although I am a specialist, she often consulted with me on other aspects of their care. She received her personality and determination from her parents, always cheerful and looking on the bright side of sometimes somber medical issues. Many family members lack the attention to details that Susan made sure were carried out.

As a medical professional, I see the growing need for caregiving on a daily basis. It is a tough job and I admire those who provide it. Many families are relegating care to institutions, such as nursing homes, assisted living facilities or memory care centers, as their needs require. However, many of these facilities cannot or do not provide all the personal attention necessary. With the continuing changes in medical care insurance coverage, families will have even more responsibilities, now and in the future. The family must help out to see that the proper care is provided.

The Gunn story is one of millions playing out in our country every day. "Matters of the Heart" is a compelling reading for any current or future caregiver. There is much to learn and Susan has much to share.

Sincerely,
James A. Richardson, M.D., PhD., F.A.C.C.

Chapter One
Matters Of The Heart

This Texas raised girl was enjoying living in Southern California but my aging parents were beginning to have health issues. I felt my California dreaming time might be coming to a close as I joined an annual July 4th camping trip to the Sierras with my group of friends. Some friends who had moved away to the San Francisco area had even come down to be with us. There was still snow in the mountains and the scenery was breathtaking, as we left early one morning for a hike to a nearby lake.

Various friends in the group knew that I was considering moving back to Texas and we talked about it going up the trail. We stopped for lunch at a beautiful snow melt stream, with a great view. As others began to pack up to keep going up the trail, I felt a true tug to stay behind and pray about whether I was to move or not.

I knew they would return in a few hours on the same trail, so I sent the small group of 20 hiker friends on their way to the mountain lake. It was so quiet and peaceful after they continued on, that I climbed one of the rocks, with my back against the mountain, for the ultimate view of the rough valley floor below, as I wondered why I would want to move away from this majestic view.

The peace and quiet was soon shattered by a young child's screams, up the mountain, getting closer and closer. I turned and looked up the rough mountainside to see a young boy running through the brush, wide eyed and flailing his arms wildly. Crawling down off my rock, I yelled at him to stay there.

I quickly took off my socks and hiking boots, found a long bare stick and waded across the cold snow melt stream to the boy. He was talking excitedly, first explaining that he was lost and that if he had not found anyone, he had already decided he would crawl up against one of the rocks for shelter at night. He was not sure what he would eat but that he would find something and he was not worried about water because there was still snow.

It took several minutes of calming him down to even get his name. After determining "Steve" had been lost long enough for his imagination to run wild, I realized I did not have a map. I did not need one if I was just going to stay put and contemplate the rest of my life.

Now, however, I realized a map would have been helpful to return Steve to safety.

When you are in the wilderness and you do not know where to go, you are to stay in place. I knew that my friends would be returning on the trail and, should we not have anyone else pass by before then, we could then take Steve back to his family, when we had the map to do so.

Steve and I spent the next few hours together talking and telling stories. He was camping with his dad; and his mom was going to be real mad. He was eight years old and he went to church with the neighbors sometimes. He had been going back to their campsite to change into his swimsuit and he got lost. And he was a Chicago Bulls fan, as evidenced by his ball cap.

We talked about school, what he liked and did not like, all the while, looking up the mountain from where he had come down, sitting or leaning on my rock. Then he asked why I had stayed behind and not gone with my friends.

Parts of that day are vague now after twenty three years, including his name. But this part is etched in my memory. We were both looking up the mountain.

To his question, I simply replied, "I have some important life decisions to make."

In his sweet eight year old voice, he inquired, "What do you have to decide?"

"Whether to move from California or not."

"Where would you move?"

"Texas."

"Oh, that's a long ways a way."

"Yep."

Pause. Then Steve said, "Why would you move?"

Deep breath.

"My parents live in Texas. That's where I moved to California from. My dad got sick and I might need to go back to help both my parents. They are getting pretty old and none of my brothers or sister live in Texas either."

Another pause. "You were here when I needed you to help me. You should go home where they need you to help them."

Under my breath, "Out of the mouths of babes..."

Long pause. It is obvious he was contemplatively thinking.

"Do you have kids?" he asked.

Another sigh. "No, I'm still single. I haven't gotten married."

"Why haven't you gotten married?"

"Great question."

Steve turns now and faces me, "You should get married and have kids because you would be a really great mom. But, you should still move home to help your mom and dad."

I was expecting an answer to the question on whether to move. I was not expecting the answer to be from an eight year old lost boy in the Sierras.

Steve and I talked for close to three hours. I was beginning to be concerned that no one was coming back at that point, that we would both be lost and huddled against the rocks but shortly after that completely bizarre thought crossed my mind, I saw a man hiking down the mountain with a small jacket in his hand.

He looked at me with questioning eyes but I quickly explained the no map problem, that my friends had gone up the trail with the map and would soon be back. Steve said he recognized him from the campsite next to theirs and they started the climb back up the mountain.

Not long after Steve and the man left, a park ranger on horseback came through looking for him. When I told him the story, he looked the direction to where Steve would have continued running and said, "If he had gotten past you, there is nothing but wilderness out there. He might have ended up in some serious trouble. Good thing you stayed behind from your friends."

I looked to where he had gazed and he was right. It was pretty rough looking. But I also knew I was not there by mistake, but by design. God used my parents to get me to hang back from hiking up the mountain, to save Steve from greater danger. Then God blessed me by giving me an answer through a sweet eight year old voice.

My friends returned shortly after the park ranger left, with all of them talking excitedly. It seems, this little boy went missing just before they got to the top of the mountain, from a campsite area. The dad was frantic, as were some of the other campers who were looking for the boy.

My friends got the dad and other campers together to pray for the boy's safety. But no one knew what that answer was going to be. When they returned, all 20 of them were trying to tell me about it at once. I was smiling when I realized I was an answer too. I stated quietly,
"His name was Steve. And, he loves the Chicago Bulls."

The silence was deafening as the answer soaked in. I paused as the questions started coming.

"You found him?" "He was here?" "Was he ok?"

"He found me. Yes, he was here. He was scared but he was ok. And, according to Steve, I need to move home to help my parents like I helped him."

Caregiving is an act of caring for your elderly loved ones, that consumes time, energy, resources, emotion, every aspect of the one giving care. It can be the most loving act of service for a loved one nearing the end of their long life.

It both interrupts and blesses your life. I experienced the broadest range of emotions that I had ever experienced thus far in my sixty years, beginning at age thirty-eight. It is something, quite frankly, that we hope we will never have to do but yet, when faced with the inevitable, we choose to dive into caregiving.

CAREGIVING: "Caregiving is the act of providing unpaid assistance and support to family members or acquaintances who have physical, psychological, or developmental needs. Caring for others generally takes on three forms: instrumental, emotional, and informational caring. Instrumental help includes activities such as shopping for someone who is disabled or cleaning for an elderly parent. Caregiving also involves a great deal of emotional support, which may include listening, counseling, and companionship. Finally, part of caring for others may be informational in nature, such as learning how to alter the living environment of someone in the first stages of dementia."[1]

I had no idea what I was getting into when moving home to provide care for my parents. Caregiving was a foreign thought to me in 1995. In my teenage years, my church choir had sung at plenty of nursing homes. It was then I made the decision that I did not want my parents to live in a nursing home if at all possible.

Though my grandmom had cared for her father and my mom cared for her mother, for some reason, I failed to realize nor consider that this generational opportunity would not bypass me.

Then Daddy had a heart attack. No siblings lived in the same state anymore. I felt someone needed to be close by to help with any care that needed to be provided as they grew older.

As it turned out, I was the youngest and unattached (single) sibling. All my other siblings were older, married, had kids, fully entrenched in their lives and where they lived. At the time I had been living in Southern California for six years and it seemed sensible to return to Texas. It was the least intrusive for me to do so and I knew it was illogical to have them move to California to me, away from all their friends.

Everything moved fast, decisions had to be made, and it made sense. I could not foresee truly what I was agreeing to, and how it would shape my life and my parent's lives forever.

I had no forewarning, no preparation, no words of wisdom about the myriad of emotions I would experience over the sixteen years of caregiving and through subsequent years as well. I was most often overwhelmed with all the decisions that I had to make. I made them often for four very independent, stubborn adults. Myself included. Every decision I made in life, big and small, had to be filtered first through all my caregiving responsibilities.

Over sixteen years, for three elderly ones, there were 3 rehabs, 3 nursing homes, 18 emergency room visits, 6 intensive care visits, 15 hospital stays, and a minimum of 1328 healthcare office visits, including optometrists, ophthalmologists, audiologists, dentists, oral surgeons, allergist, neurologists, urologists, cardiologists, pulmonologists, surgeons, orthopedists, gastroenterologist, otolaryngologist, internists, dermatologist, podiatrist, nephrologist, gynecologists and primary care physicians.

I think the only type of doctor not seen in those sixteen years was a pediatrician!

MATTER:
Everything around you.
Everything that has mass and takes up space.
The amount of stuff (big and small) in an object.

OBJECT:
The end toward which effort or action is directed; a goal; a purpose.

If matter is everything that takes up space, then caregiving is truly matter. The emotions that are consumed when caregiving, the energy expended, the communication required, the extensive planning – the amount of stuff in caregiving is overwhelming. The time it devours. The space it occupies is your heart. Every single aspect of your heart.

Caregiving responsibilities expand just as mass and matter expands.

When making any plans for anything in your life, it is the first thing that must be considered. Vacation? Probably not. Travels for business? Compounded difficulty. How to still work and catch doctors during a hospital stay is an art form. Everything in life is juggled, with endless frustrations a real possibility. Those sixteen years were simply the most difficult of my 60 years thus far.

They required sacrifice, flexibility, patience, honesty, a deep running faith and an abundance of love.

I felt inadequate, lost, disappointed, exhausted, heartbroken, trapped and angry – sometimes all at the same time.

I always had to think about worst case scenarios, planning ahead, just in case. What-ifs consumed me. Without fail, I charged my cell phones at night because I never knew if the next day would include a hospital run. It was a gut wrenching experience.

Yet, I would not have done it any other way.

I loved my parents. Were they simply the best parents in the world, as some think? Not a chance. My parents made plenty of mistakes growing up, which required forgiveness on my part or I would not have been able to be there for them.

The parents that raised me were not the same parents that I cared for – they grew up as well. But, they were still the parents that I loved.

My caregiving was not perfect either. I had absolutely no clue what I was doing. In 1995, caregiving was not a hot topic. Nobody talked about it. There was no manual or guidebook. Mom used to fret over what we needed to do. My constant reply was, "I don't know what to do either, Mom, but we'll figure it out together."

I guess in many ways then, **caregiving was simply coming alongside my parents as they grew older, to walk with them to the end.** I did not take over anything until they could not do whatever it was any longer.

We were a team. When they were more able, they participated in their daily routine. As they grew less able, greater care was required. I always knew it was going to get worse, not better.

Harder, never easier.

Requires more time, not less.

And it did.

In the midst of all the heartache times, we built great memories.

Game playing was brutally competitive in our family. Killer Uno brought tears to many participants' eyes. Hand-And-Foot, Dominoes, Mexican Train, Rummikub™, 42, Spades - we played them all! We played games to the end, very competitively. Mom would always start off by saying "I'm not sure I remember how to play this game," then beat the crud out of all of us. Every time.

They were very socially active – that helped keep some sense of sanity in the midst of the other completely insane times.

My heart was tested, time and time again. Work did provide some kind of counterbalance. Being with friends - a saving grace. The tendency was to isolate myself for a few captured quiet moments. Through exhaustion, friends would coerce me to join them in a night out. Just getting dressed up to go out seemed a chore but I was always glad I did. I needed my friends.

Yes, sometimes caring for parents, who will eventually die, is depressing. There. I said it. The end goal is not that they will live a gazillion more years. The end goal is to have them enjoy what remainder of life there will be to the fullest.

It was hard.

Knowing their laughter would not always be with me. Knowing that their shared wisdom would not always be available.

Knowing that their countless repeated stories would never be repeated again. Knowing that someday, the house would be really quiet. Knowing that someday, you would want to pick up the phone and share with them some exciting news.

For me, they were the greatest supporters of my business. My most important cheerleaders. Members of my board. Board meetings were held at David's BBQ Restaurant down the street over fried okra. But they always wanted to hear what was going on in my business. I miss that immensely.

It has been five years since Mom passed away and this book has been in process for the nine years since Dad passed away. It is a heart endeavor and requires the deepest heart wrenching process to share with you, the same struggles you may encounter when caregiving your loved one.

I can just hear my dad say, "What's taking you so long? Get 'er done!"

There are many published books on how to give care for the elderly loved ones in our life but so few books on the heart that is required in caregiving. I am certainly not an expert.

Realistically, no book could ever possibly contain all the answers you need to provide care for your elderly one, as all circumstances are vastly different and all families vastly unique.

This book is about my journey and the journey of some of my friends, what we have learned in the process and some suggestions that may help you. I have been brutally honest and extremely vulnerable in the writing of what happened. I have invited you to read about the good, the bad and the ugly side of caregiving.

I recommend journaling your thoughts at the end of each chapter, then in the back of the book are questions for you to consider further. This is my journey but you are reading it because of your own journey in caregiving. In your journal, write your own stories and memories.

Anyone that knows me knows I can tell a story for anything and everything. I learned this skill from Dad. He could truly spin a yarn. I think most of them were true. In this book, I stick to the true ones to make it real for you. And there are so many more stories where those came from!

Some stories I may change the names to protect the innocent or the guilty. Some stories are not my own but a friend's situation that would be helpful for you to know.

Some stories were hard to write. All stories have left me completely vulnerable. Some days, it felt like I was standing completely naked in front of this book, stripped of anything previously labeled private.

Each story, each event, I asked myself what Mom would have said about what I was writing. Dad would not have cared. Mom would. The book you are reading is the result of many, many edits, and many peer reviews but there will still be many times you will be uncomfortable reading my journey. It is okay. I included the uncomfortable stories because so many of you will experience similar situations.

My hope is, in the reading, you will relate and be encouraged, you will become aware and be prepared, that in the way I walked beside my parents that I will walk beside you.

I get it. I truly get it.

Caregiving will indeed affect every aspect of your heart. I do not pretend to know everything about caregiving but just to share what my heart experienced in the process.

Caregiving is the matter that consumes your heart and your life.

Chapter Two
Sacrifice: The Call & The Purpose

It all started with a phone call.

I was single and thirty-eight years old, living in Southern California in 1993 and it was my weekly phone call to check in with my eighty and seventy-nine year old parents, still living in the Texas homestead.

"Well, we did not want to alarm you but we just got home from the hospital. Your dad had a slight heart attack but he's ok. There's nothing to be concerned about."

Seriously?

A slight heart attack is about the same level as a slight stroke, I thought. I resisted the temptation to cancel my calendar the following week and fly home but deep down in my gut, I knew that something big in my life was about to change.

I knew I was about to be a third generation family member to take care of their elderly parents.

My great granddad moved in with my grandparents. Mom did not remember much of caring for him but remembered that it just seemed natural to have him live with their family.

It just seemed natural that my grandmom came to live with us when she could no longer live alone. It was terribly hard for her to leave her friends but Mom promised to take her back for visits, which she did faithfully.

Through the loving care they gave my maternal grandmom, my parents modeled the behavior they wanted in being cared for in their elderly years – lovingly, with patience and gentleness.

Then that phone call.

Mom and Dad still lived in the home Dad built in Arlington, Texas, the year before I was born. They were deeply involved in their Sunday School class, bridge group and many other community and social endeavors.

I had moved to Southern California several years before and was busy living a single's life in my 30s. I had a great job I loved, settled with fun friends, and was truly enjoying all the benefits of a beach and a ski slope just a car ride away.

My youngest brother and his family lived near our parents until a job promotion moved them to Pennsylvania. My sister and my oldest brother lived out of state with their families. We were all living our own lives, completely unaware it was all about to change.

Then that "slight heart attack" phone call.

As I hung up the phone, the thought was planted. Maybe I should move home? They were getting up there in age. It was a question I began to contemplate the answer to as I began to consider possibilities.

My parents did not say anything. They never suggested my moving home, never implied I should. I just started evaluating the situation: I was the only one who could uproot and go home.

Just as quickly as I considered the option, the question, "Why do I have to move?" would envelope me. "Why me?"

I asked that question quite a bit from that point forward. I really enjoyed my life in California but I always knew I would not be there forever.

That phone call was in early June. I spent the next few weeks evaluating my options, talking to friends, talking with my bosses at work and praying about it. It was not an easy decision to uproot and move back.

Though my company was reluctant to lose me from corporate headquarters, there was an option to open a newer branch in Houston, Texas. They would pay for the move, I would take a slight change in compensation and I would be out of the protective umbrella of a corporate environment, so I was warned.

I had the best solid group of friends, who were also single, from my church. We would go play beach volleyball on Sundays, we would go on bike rides on the thousands of available bike paths, we would take regular camping trips into the mountains, we would meet up during the week for dinners or gather at someone's house to watch a football game. We were all "growing up" as adults together.

I hated to lose them in the move.

Here were my choices as I understood them:

1. Do nothing. After all, it was just a "slight" heart attack.

2. Plan to move in 5 years.

3. Transfer or quit my job and move back home before I was seriously needed.

Then I went camping in the Sierras with my friends and met a young wise man named Steve.

The next month, I moved to Houston, Texas for a new position with my company. At least I would be in the same state, just a four hour car ride away. Just over a year later, Dad had a more serious heart attack that landed him in Intensive Care for almost a month. I was driving back and forth from Houston to Arlington, with both my job and my sanity suffering. After that heart attack, I realized I needed to be in the same town.

I believe things happen for a reason. I was warned prior to transferring from the California home office that there were imminent layoffs in the future, that I would be unprotected should I move. They were correct – my position in Houston was eliminated, allowing me to move back home to Arlington. It all worked out, and though I felt the financial sacrifice quite quickly, that commitment and sacrifice to my parents within a couple of years allowed me to start my own business.

Again, things happen for a reason.

My commitment to caring for my parents, completely changed life as I had grown to love it. Because of my willingness to sacrifice, I was able to commit to caring for them. Sacrifice and commitment often worked in tandem, cropping up over and over again in the years of caregiving. There was often a sacrifice of plans, vacations, and even business. I had no idea the amount of personal sacrifice that would be required of me.

And it all started with that phone call.

I had another decision to make when I moved back to Arlington - live in the very small guest house built for my grandmom, in the back yard of my parent's property, or buy my own house. I had already begun taking care of some things with their house and caring for two properties did not appeal to me. At this point, I did not have a job, so into the guest house, I moved. The very very very small guest house.

Living in that very very small guest house, with very very small bills, allowed me to begin my own business a very few short years later. Listening to the morning news while getting ready to go to work at CompUSA™ where I was teaching business software courses on Windows 3.1™ and the newly launched Windows 95™, I heard an interview with a gentleman who was close in age to myself (39 yrs old) about how he built a business on an idea.

For some reason, that resonated with me. First, I thought how cool that he had such a great idea but then how even more cool that he could turn that idea into earning a living! Little did I realize I was about to do the same thing.

I knew I needed to work with a flexible schedule and that the standard career positions I had over the years would never work. Up to this point, I had been in sales management, with travel.

I was lured from CompUSA™ to work with a dental automation company, where I worked for one year. I had been very fortunate to have some amazing businessmen, including my dad, encourage me to branch out on my own. So, I did.

I began teaching dentists, doctors, veterinarians and chiropractors how to organize their financial information in QuickBooks™ in a more understandable way. I had been using Quicken™ since it was DOS and my first edited/written CompUSA™ QuickBooks™ book was for QuickBooks 2.0™.

That was 22 versions ago.

In the beginning, I would travel to their practices but what a blessing the internet became! Remote training via a browser through the internet gave me the capability to still be close to my parents. Just about the time their need for care increased, the remote training became a possibility.

Throughout the sixteen years of caregiving, there were many conscious decisions of sacrifice. The sacrifice was most often making a career decision based on the needs of another. As you will, over and over and over again.

Many times, I wanted to simply walk away. Those were the times I was overwhelmed, with little or no help. I was never aware of all the adjustments that would be made when I first committed to moving home. I was clueless. I certainly never knew that commitment was to be for sixteen years.

Years before, while I was in college, the newscast highlighted the average life expectancy was sixty-five years old. It had been eleven years since I heard the average life expectancy but they were already past it at 79. I somehow concluded my caregiving would only be needed for a few short years at most. I was wrong.

I will never get back those sixteen years. I never married. I never had children. Who knows if I would have or not, had I had the time to actually date. I do not blame my parents as it is a choice I made. Any spare time I had was consumed by parents or working. When I first moved home, I went camping with friends, rode bikes, went to the gym, was active in my church. Those last seven years, there was very little time and very little energy left over for me or anyone else.

I learned I had to leave town to get work completed, such as all the technical books I wrote during those years. I bought into a timeshare condo near the beach in South Texas and would sequester myself there to write every fall when the new QuickBooks™ software would come out.

Those times away were not without incident either but whatever sibling, niece or nephew was in town, would have to help. During the seven hour drive south, I would try to let the stress of caregiving fall away, mile by mile and decompress, so that I could focus on what I needed to accomplish when I arrived.

The Unknown

How does someone decide to be the caregiver for their parents?

Let me first say, you will never know how long or short
your commitment will be. There is no crystal ball that can give you any
insight as to what is down the road. You will never know how many storms
there are ahead or how many valleys will need traversing.

When you make a commitment, you must know, as a caregiver, you are
branching out into the vast UNKNOWN. It is probably the vaguest decision
you will ever make, over and over again. It is a decision that you will question
in your head often, your friends will verbally challenge you with, and your
relatives may often not support.

Your life will be interrupted repeatedly. You may incur financial difficulty
from providing care for a parent. My ability to work was often interrupted
and when you own your own business and do not work, no one pays you sick
pay or vacation pay.

Think long and hard about your commitment. Caregiving is not for the faint
at heart and should not be entered into lightly. Commitment and sacrifice
walk hand in hand throughout caregiving.

You have a choice to make. You can certainly say no to being the primary
caregiver but understand you are saying no to decisions regarding the
future care of your elderly loved one. Be sure you are making an informed
decision. As far as caregiving is concerned, ignorance is not bliss. It is simply
ignorance.

> Talk with your elderly loved one. Talk with your spouse.
> Talk with your siblings. Talk with your mentors.
> Talk with your friends. Talk with your boss. Talk with your co-workers.
> Talk with someone else who is in the midst of caregiving.

Why talk to everyone in your life?

Various people are involved in various aspects of your life and see you from a completely different perspective than the others. Though you think it will not, caregiving affects everyone in your life, all relationships, at all levels. You are making sure you are covering all the bases and have thought about all the "knowns" at this point.

Meeting with your siblings gives everyone an opportunity to share their hearts and any concerns. You must make this decision with as much information as possible. This decision will affect the rest of your parent's lives, the rest of your sibling's lives and the rest of your life. Even if the caregiving is short term, the impact is life long.

There is no instruction manual in caregiving for your elderly loved ones. The mere word does imply giving care. Care. It starts with caring. Because you care, you will commit and sacrifice many aspects of your future. Just be prepared. And remember to care.

The purpose in caregiving is to provide care for whatever is needed, for however long it is needed. If you decided you cannot be the primary caregiver, be supportive, not judgmental. Be encouraging, not critical.

Be the reliever, the backup, the cavalry in time of need. Call and see if you can relieve the primary caregiver for a few days, a week or longer. Understand the caregiver cannot make any travel plans without making arrangements. You can help, even if you are not the primary caregiver.

For example, a friend of mine is not her mom's primary caregiver. She and her sister have worked out a plan where she comes to relieve her sister four to six times a year. Their mom is in a nursing home and getting excellent care.

While my friend is in town, her sister is on "vacation." She does not even stay with her sister because they learned all they would do is talk about their mom. Her sister needed a true break so now they get together for dinner one night while she is in town.

My friend feels guilty she is unable to be available more often but she is here at every holiday, breaks and vacations. Her sister is thankful for the breaks she gets because their brother lives much farther away and is unable to come as often.

Caring for your elderly loved one is not restricted to the primary caregiver. It is required of all of us, in some degree or another.

Chapter Three
Forgiveness: For Past Imperfections

Do you harbor resentment against a family member, a parent or grandparent, for events of the past?

Are you still angry about whatever happened in your childhood?

Does it spill over to resentment in having to care for them?

Harboring unforgiveness against your elderly one will affect your caregiving, your sanity and your perseverance.

Caregiving requires a discipline of the heart that, quite frankly, you might not feel like giving.

Forgiveness on your part MUST happen prior to caregiving. Nursing homes are full of residents whose children have not forgiven them. It broke my heart to hear those stories when visiting my step-grandmother in her nursing home, as a nurse relayed to me that some of the residents' children never visited their parent.

I know this happens often and I know there are typically good reasons: not living or working close by and not a good relationship being the top two reasons.

Along with all those reasons, another is a lack of forgiveness.

The older I have become, the more I truly understand this concept. The parents I cared for were not the parents who raised me. Yes, there were some similarities but we both grew up immeasurably as we aged.

My mom could be emotionally harsh my childhood years. She was not always unpleasant, which made it very similar to living with an alcoholic.

I never knew how she was going to be when I opened the back door from a day at school. I did not and could not trust her emotions.

We did not have a very good relationship through my childhood years. If you had not experienced those early childhood years, you would have never guessed that the mother of my youth was the same mother I cared for the last years of her life.

My three other siblings are between 8 to 19 years older than me. The oldest brother never lived in the same home as I did. My sister left home for college when I was five. My other brother left home for college when I was ten. They never returned.

I grew up pretty much alone and was a fairly energetic child born to older parents. Mom was 42 years old and Dad was 43 years old. I was a surprise!

I was very ADD. I know I was a handful. I was truly not a clone of my older siblings. As a dear friend of my parents said, "I was an *ACTIVE* child."

I often did not measure up to the expectations of a well behaved child.

Dad occasionally intervened but even he tried to stay out of her way when she was on a rant. She could be modeling Mommy Dearest one second with me and answer the phone with a happy lilt in her voice the next second.

In my twenties, I realized they did the very best they knew how to do. They learned from their parents, who were not perfect either. My paternal grandmom passed when Dad was 13 years old. My maternal grandmom could be snippy as well.

They grew up in a similar environment and did not realize the level that the dysfunction had risen to in our own family or had become for me as a child.

It does help to put yourself in their shoes. Again, it does not excuse the behavior but aids in the forgiving process. I call myself a hormonal surge baby, premenopausal. When I turned 42, the age of Mom when she gave birth to me, I got it. Yikes.

I began the process of forgiveness in my twenties but in my forties, that forgiveness grew substantially.

Every year since, on my birthday, I have said, "Oh my gosh. When Mom was my age, she had a 3 year old, an 11 year old, an 18 year old and a 22 year old," determining how old my siblings were as well. When she was 60 years old, I was graduating from high school.

Let us be honest. Many of us grew up with turbulence behind our front doors. That turbulence affected us, in one form or another. To say we moved on completely would be a lie.

Some of us carry more baggage than others.

Some have downsized to a carry-on.

Some are still lugging trunks full of their emotional past.

Maybe your parents were amazing. Then this chapter may not be for you.

But, maybe during your childhood, your mom or dad was an alcoholic or addict.

Maybe during your childhood, your mom or dad was physically abusive.
Maybe during your childhood, your mom or dad was sexually abusive.
Maybe during your childhood, your mom or dad was emotionally abusive.
Maybe you grew up in a violent area and blame your parents.
Maybe you witnessed violence as a child.
Maybe you blame your parents for not changing your circumstances as a child.
Maybe one parent left to never return.

Blame is more than a five letter word. It implies a negative emotion and is often followed by a conscious or subconscious action.

Blame plunders years from your life.

Blame hijacks happiness from your life.

Blame shackles you from living free and loving freely.

Again, I do not have all the answers for the life hurt that you have experienced. It is your own. You own it. You must decide what to do with it.

I do know it is your choice whether to hang on to it. You can carry it around for a few more years or get to work on getting rid of it.

I became very resentful and bitter. It made me cynical of life. It made me sarcastic in very deeply hurtful ways with those I love.

Being resentful, made me full of wrath. I wore resentment well. In many ways, I was a bully. I wore that exterior as a protection from anyone else hurting me, especially my family.

I chose that route as a response to my deeply rooted, childhood hurt. I did not have to choose it and it was not until I understood that I could choose not to be resentful, that I began to change.

My faith as a Christian helped me. I knew the Lord would be with me every step of my growth.

I have a Bachelor's degree in Psychology. I have heard lots of references regarding those who have degrees in psychology. For the most part, they are true!

I was trying to figure out my family of mixed messages, where words were never trusted because the actions that followed were much stronger in the opposite direction.

I read a lot of books on various topics, which often included ideas on forgiveness and this psychology graduate also went to counseling. Counseling helped me work through some of the more difficult issues.

It required discipline on my part, to focus on what I loved about both of my parents. I chose to focus on the positive and that encouraged a response of love, compassion, and humility.

There are those out there that experienced far worse in their homes than I ever did. Some have stories of being a lifelong victim. Some have remarkable stories of overcoming.

I choose to focus on the positive memories, for they far outweigh the negative ones. The parents I took care of the last years of their life, were not the same parents that raised me. Somewhere along the way, they mellowed. They matured.

Menopause eventually ended for Mom, though some of the attributes lived on for a few years. I guess some of those habits were slow to go away.

Do you still harbor resentment against your elderly one? This will affect your caregiving and your perseverance. Consider ongoing counseling during your caregiving timespan.

You have a choice.

There is no excuse to continue to put on wrath daily and wear it.

You are only robbing yourself and those around you.

And it will sabotage your caregiving.

Chapter Four
Inadequacy: Role Changing

As I moved back to Arlington, I wondered about this new adventure I was committing to: no knowledge of what was going to happen or how long it would take, with absolutely no road map.

What job would offer flexibility to be available when it was needed?

I had worked since I was 14 years old. I had to have an income. I could not give up current and future potential earnings to care for my parents. Mom and Dad would never have asked that of me.

I did understand that primary caregiving was going to be my full time focus, but not my paying job. It was a huge responsibility, and now the roles had switched. I was now in the parental role, even though I had no experience as a parent.

In the beginning, Mom and Dad were both physically and emotionally active. They played bridge in the same couples group for over 40 years. Once a month, the couples rotated playing at each other's home. The "pot" for the winner was exorbitant - $2.00 for the winner and $.25 for the loser.

In addition to bridge, my parents would also play cribbage after their morning devotional time. The winner would brag about it until the next competition.

Mom and Dad were active members in their Sunday School class and their church for over 60 years. Dad served on the board at First United Methodist and Mom sang in the choir and played hand bells.

Mom loved to take walks, often stopping to visit friends along the street, while Dad worked in the yard or his workshop building or fixing something around the house. They both grew a vegetable garden for most of their lives. Tomatoes and green beans off the vines were canned for the year's enjoyment.

Even though my parents were still relatively independent when I first moved home, those years were special. They allowed us to build our relationship and bond for the tough times ahead, when they needed more care. It made the transition so much easier for all of us.

They told a lot of stories about their growing up years that I had never heard. Mom told stories about her mom making biscuits for homeless men that would stop by the back porch in search of food during the great depression. Granddad worked at a mill and she had ample flour to make them. It was a generous way to share her gift in cooking and her resources with the flour.

Dad told stories about being stationed in Alaska during World War II. He was an enlisted man that served in the telegraph radio room because there were not enough officers on base.

During the wee hours one morning, a coded message was received. Dad decoded it but it was still encrypted. He told the guard to go wake the commander. No one was supposed to leave the post, guard or Dad, so the guard argued but Dad felt this was really important. He had never received a message like this before.

The commander came to the radio room in his bedtime attire, saw the message and took it out of the room to his office - also not supposed to happen. He returned shortly with an already coded message and told Dad to code it again and then send it.

After it was sent, the commander leaned back and ordered coffee for both Dad and him. The commander only said with a smile, "This was big, Gunn. You'll read about this in the papers tomorrow."

The next day, the papers blasted the story about how the new Japanese warship had been sunk in Tokyo Bay. As Dad told the story, his eyes would shut periodically, as if he could still see the whole telegraphy radio room once more. I was proud of him already but it did not surprise me that he was chosen as an enlisted man to do an officer's duty. He was a man of integrity, a man who held his commitment and a man who could be trusted, apparently even during his younger years.

During those early caregiving years, I drove them to Tennessee and Mississippi for a week of "grave digging." Mom was a genealogist and still actively keeping up with long lost dead relatives. Inevitably, she would ask someone their last name and tie it in with someone in our family tree.

My childhood family vacations were spent doing research in county courthouse basements, reviewing old documents on microfiche and determining how old someone was when they died by reading their tombstones in the overgrown cemeteries. My true goal was to determine how fast you can spin a microfiche reel until the librarian gave me the evil eye to make me stop.

Mom had written and published three books on the Gunn lineage, Kendrick lineage and the Fitzgerald lineage. All three are in the Library of Congress and the Gunn book is in the Gunn Clan Heritage Centre and Museum in Latheron, Scotland.

The trip to Mississippi was a fun last research jaunt. It always bothered Mom that she never found where her great grandfather Kendrick was buried after he was injured during the Civil War battle of Shiloh. He had moved his family to Louisiana to keep them safe from harm, and then returned to protect their small farm in Tennessee. He was injured but relatives said he just wanted to get back to his family, and left before he was healed.

We did not find his grave that trip but it was not for lack of dusty basements, talking to many long lost "relatives" or combing through knee high weeds at an off the beaten path cemetery. Years after that trip, she would say, "Do you think when I get to heaven that I'll find out where he was buried?" I would reply, "Heck, Mom. At that point, you will meet him, so it won't matter where he is buried!"

As much as Mom loved genealogical research, Dad loved fishing. When Dad was building houses, it was not uncommon for his business partner and him to decide that they had built all they could that day and leave at noon for the lake. Just about the time I was ready to start skiing behind our ski boat, Dad sold it and bought an aluminum fishing boat. No, I'm not bitter.

Instead of skiing an enjoyable day on the lake, I sat in an aluminum fishing boat, on a seriously way too early morning.   The last fishing trip I took with him on the boat, we sat for seven hours before he loudly proclaimed, "I know what we aren't doing right!"

Smiling at me, he put his pole down, leaned over the side of the boat and started tapping the side, chanting in a high sing song voice, "Here fishy fishy. [pause] Here fishy fishy. [pause] Here fishy fishy."

Other boats nearby had noticeable shoulders moving up and down from their laughter, while I was rolling my eyes and shaking my head.

Dad picked up his pole again, saying, "There. That should do it." It was not four minutes after he put his pole back in the water that he caught a fish.

It made me a believer, so I tried the same thing. The fish must have caught on because they were not falling for that same gimmick twice. I can still hear him singing that chant! We buried him with a fishing lure in his pocket.

They both loved to read and, when I first began caring for them, their eyes were still good. When we discovered the murder mystery writer Sue Grafton wrote the alphabet books (A is for Alibi©), we made a chart" A, B, C, D...." and three columns "F, B, S" (Floyd, Beth, Su) and passed the books around until we had read all she had written up to that point in the alphabet.

Those were all formative years, building a foundation for the care in their not so distant future.

Switching Roles

When I use the term "elderly" in this book, I am implying an older aged adult. There is not one set age that one suddenly attains "elderly" status. Some younger adults believe age 60 is elderly. I resent AND reject that thought. When I state "elderly" throughout this book, though, I am implying an aging adult who is physical and mental capabilities are slowly diminishing. That could happen at 65 years old or not until 90 years old.

As my parents slowly grew older, I became the parent. Because we had invested time into our relationship as adults, spending time talking and lots of time laughing with and at each other, the transition from child to parent was as smooth as it ever could be.

Slowly through the years, I began doing the tasks they had been doing. I realized at some point, I would be doing it all, so I was careful not to do anything that they were still capable of doing themselves.

This was vitally important. **I wanted them to still have purpose in their lives, to be able to do as much as they could and wanted to, for as long as they could.** To be honest, I also did not want to do everything. If they could still do some things for themselves, why should I take on that responsibility?

I had a conversation with Dad while grilling outside one day about driving. I asked if he still felt comfortable driving, as he had recently turned 88. We discussed it as a matter of fact, without any defensiveness or emotion, long before I felt he would actually need to give up driving. In my conversation, I allowed him to have the wisdom to know when it would be time to NOT drive.

I did ask him not to give me grief when it came time for him to quit driving. I said I hoped I would not have to ask for the keys. He told me that conversation would not go over very well and I knew it would not. I think he remembered that conversation, when four years later, about two years before he passed away, he told my youngest brother and me to sell the car.

However, I did NOT have that conversation with my Mom, who was pretty upset that we would not let her drive any longer. She told all her friends that she was still perfectly capable of driving but that we would not let her drive. It was mostly my fault, she would tell her friends. I could take the blame just fine because I knew we were potentially saving other people's lives and her own!

One friend, whose elderly parent's dementia had worsened, took the car home so it would not be driven. The elderly one forgot the son had taken the car home to sell and reported it stolen to the police. The son was surprised when the police, with lights on, were in front of his house, with questions regarding the stolen car in the driveway.

As I slowly became the parent, they slowly became more like children. **My frustration became greatest when I expected them to still make decisions as a parent or an adult.** It was hard to grasp the reality that they no longer could make decisions the same way as they had at one time.

It was frustrating to them as well.

I became the nurse, the cook, the housekeeper, the organizer, the meeting planner, the personal shopper, the groundskeeper, the diffuser, the go-between, the friend, the patient advocate, the counselor, all while running my own business.

I also became the parent. Slowly, little by little, they gave their roles up as a parent or adult, and I became the caregiver.

What role was left for them as I became the parent?

What was their purpose now?

Losing Purpose

An elderly person often becomes desperate to determine their purpose. They are now retired, which previously often defined their purpose. Their lives become less active; they become frustrated, lonely and afraid of the unknown - future and death. They are often depressed and confused by something new, different and out of the routine they are accustomed.

The elderly one may be embarrassed about things they cannot control and processing information is much slower. Foods previously loved and devoured do not taste the same and they cannot see or hear as well as they used to.

They most often do not realize that their decision-making ability has significantly diminished. They never seem to understand the degree to which it has diminished. Where it is obvious to everyone else, it is not obvious to them.

Population Health Expert Archana Singh-Manoux, PhD states that memory, reasoning and comprehension can begin to decline as early as age 45. [1]

A University of Virginia study suggests cognitive capabilities slowly decline beginning at age 27, with "a notable decline in certain measures of abstract reasoning, brain speed and in puzzle-solving." "Accumulated knowledge skills, such as improvement of vocabulary and general knowledge, actually increase at least until the age of 60."[2]

A male's cognitive function declines differently than a female's. Men's cognitive function declines less than women's by 1% in 45 to 49 years old. During 65 to 70 years old, men decline 3% more than women.

Though these studies are important, I believe they cannot rule out the person's personal purpose in life as it directly relates to a cognitive decline. A person's purpose motivates them to live, even as their bodies are declining.

Maslow's Hierarchy of Needs

Abraham Maslow has certainly had his share of critics since he first introduced his Theory of Human Motivation in 1943[3].

He believed that advanced motivational needs are built upon foundational motivational needs. If the foundational motivational needs are not met, we are then not motivated to obtain the more advanced needs.

Basically, in Maslow's theory, there are five different levels of motivational needs:

Physiological - the most foundational need, this includes: air, food, drink, shelter, warmth, sex, sleep

Security - protection from elements, security, order, law, stability, etc.

Social - friendship, intimacy, affection and love from work, family, friends, and romantic relationships

Esteem - achievement, mastery, independence, status, dominance, prestige, responsibility, etc.

Self-Actualization - realizing personal potential, self-fulfillment, seeking personal growth and peak experiences

One level provides support for the level above. Lower motivational needs must be satisfied before higher motivational needs are striven. Progress to satisfy higher needs may be interrupted in the failure of a lower need.

Much research and information has been written subsequently to validate the Hierarchy of Needs theory but my purpose here is to give credence to what I have seen in the aging process itself – a reshuffling of motivational needs in various stages, how this relates to the quality of care needed for the elderly and how it affects their sense of purpose.

Sadly, I have seen many of these motivational needs ignored in caring for our elderly and, in others, ignored in the caregiver. Not all people, including the elderly, will work through all the Hierarchy of Needs. For instance, some will experience a life change in family status (divorce, death of spouse or child or friend) that could interrupt a sense of belonging. A life change could affect a "Security Need" or interrupt a "Physiological Need".

As we age, many of these foundational needs require a caregiver or oversight of the elderly in order to be met, such as Physiological Needs and Safety and Security Needs. In fact, these two are pretty inseparable, as we age and become more dependent upon care.

Let's take a deeper look at how these motivational needs may affect your elderly loved one.

Physiological Needs: Air, Food, Water, Shelter, Clothing, Sleep

Basic physiological functions are necessary for our survival and they take on different meanings in the elder years. It was not Maslow's original intent but relevant nonetheless.

From a young age, we are taught to provide for ourselves these basic physiological functions. The elderly need them to survive but as they grow older, through a diminished cognitive capability, attaining them is sometimes just beyond their reach.

Air

Air is in ample supply but Dad needed a little extra oxygen. Getting him to wear his oxygen was often a battle, mostly at the beginning because he was embarrassed to carry it. But, as he needed it more, he carried it with fewer battles. As I previously discussed, our cognitive capability can be diminished from a lack of oxygen, which feeds our brain. Checking O2 levels can be important, especially for those with Chronic Obstructive

Pulmonary Disease (COPD), cardiac disease or allergies, such as asthma, in elderly patients. There are portable O2 monitors that can be purchased for a relatively low price that fit on the tip of the index finger.

Some basic processes are often forgotten, like breathing deeply, as well as drinking enough water. Mom's blood pressure readings were most often abnormally high but truly too high because she would hold her breath as someone was taking her blood pressure. Elderly skin is thin and Mom said it hurt to have the blood pressure cuff around her arm. She did not even realize she was holding her breath but anytime she was in pain, she held her breath. I learned to stand next to her, reminding her to breathe and rubbing her other arm.

Fresh air is equally important, such as taking walks or a simple change in scenery with a drive around town or a country road long unexplored. Changing the scenery lowers the stress level which allows for longer deeper breathing. We practiced the same deep breathing exercises at home that they taught in the hospital.

Water

Mom and Dad did not want to drink too much water because they would have to get up and go to the bathroom more often. Arguments always ensued. Dad was especially annoyed with me. He was on diuretics which made the water go straight through him. When aging, kidney function also begins to decline, as well as the body's ability to keep itself hydrated.

Water bottles solved the vague response to the "how much water have you drank today" question. And, as the water bottles sat on the table by my parent's recliners, they served as a visual reminder to drink water. Mom did get sneaky by filling her water bottle up, telling me she had already "filled up" her bottle so I would think she had drank quite a bit. We also kept fruit available to eat.

In the reversal of roles, even reminding Mom to drink more water seemed unnecessary – she should know she needs to drink more water but that was not the case. I would subtly do the skin test – pull up skin from their arm and see how quickly it returned to where I pulled it from. If it did not return to normal within a few seconds, they were dehydrated.

Food

Eating was an issue with Dad. The medicines he was taking tainted his taste buds so that nothing tasted good. He would come to the table to eat a well-balanced meal and state, "I'm not going to eat it." Yes, the child (me) became the parent as I replied, "Oh yes. You are going to eat it. This is not a cafeteria and this food is good for your health."

The bargaining for five bites of this and four bites of that followed. I started sautéing onions or slow boiling vanilla and water to get his salivary glands going just before dinner. Other times, I would mix one High Protein Ensure™, two tablespoons of peanut butter and two scoops of vanilla Blue Bell™ ice cream. He would eat anything with peanut butter, so I bought a whole bag of peanut butter snacks and put it by his recliner. Diabetes was not a problem, but malnutrition was.

I am so thankful for Meals On Wheels™. What a great organization to provide meals to those that not only have limited funds but limited capability to cook those meals for themselves. When one might have cooked for a household in younger years, one will often not cook for themselves alone. Several of my parents' friends volunteered with this organization for many years. I think they were planting seeds for when they would need the crop!

In the midst of negotiating with my parents, my pastor said something that struck me about choosing our battles. There are big fish and small fish. Sometimes, the arguments we pick are truly small fish - not worth the trouble. Throw the small fish back and leave it alone. Wait for a big fish. If you battle on every level, with big and small fish, you live in a constant state of challenge and the energy spent is not worth it.

I had to learn to choose my battles. Some things truly were not worth arguing over but I would not negotiate over something that would alter their health or wellbeing. Everything else was negotiable.

Clothing

They were both still able to clothe themselves, sometimes with a little help, but remembering to bathe or change clothes became an issue with Mom her last year. Honestly, there were days she stunk. Incontinence was a problem, which should have prompted her to shower daily. Many friends have told me similar stories about their parent's personal hygiene.

That conversation had to be delicate because I truly wanted to preserve her dignity. After determining she had not bathed in several days, I negotiated an every other day shower, no exceptions and began to make sure she followed through with her commitment.

Sleep

Dad wanted to stay in bed and sleep more often than be up the last few years of his life. Mom would bound out of bed and nag him until he got up. On those few occasions when that would not work, I would get a phone call. I would then do to him what he did to me when I was young, by turning on the radio loudly in his room, even louder because they were hard of hearing. Most often, he would see me coming and start moving towards getting out of bed, with a snarky grin.

The more sedentary the elderly one's lifestyle, the harder it is to sleep through the night. If they take a nap during the day, it also affects their evening time sleep. Keeping a daily schedule, i.e. awaken at the same time with bedtime the same, etc, helps attain a restful evening sleep, as well.

Mom was having some difficulty sleeping at one point. She told me that she never took naps during the day, "like your father did." The next day, I walked in to her lying in her recliner, mouth gapping open and her snoring away loudly.

Safety & Security Needs: Health, Finances, Property, Stability & Consistency

Built upon our Physiological Needs, Safety and Security is also most often overseen by the caregiver.

Health

Health is a complex subject for aging. As we get older, we take longer to heal for even the smallest offenses. A life well cared for in adulthood provides a better foundation for a healthy elderly life, but there are absolutely no guarantees. Eating nutritious well-balanced meals, exercise and good rest are important throughout our entire lives, childhood thru elderly years.

Poor health can contribute to a more rapid decline. Inflammation, hormonal imbalances and oxidative stress, such as asthma, can hasten the decline.

Mom had always taken care of herself by being active. She loved to walk, she ate healthy, and never let her weight get out of control. She aged relatively easy, with only mild dementia that was most often shown in her short term memory - what she had to eat, what she had done the night before, or what conversation she had had with whom.

Dad smoked from his teens to 65 years old. He was on oxygen the last few years of his life. His decline was most certainly less than it would have been had he not had a job where he got constant exercise as a home builder. He worked hard outdoors and played outdoors in fishing and camping.

Urinary tract infections (UTI) are very common in elderly women and can cause sudden changes in behavior, severe disorientation, low energy, constipation and pain. It is the second most common infection of all women and can cause sepsis if left untreated. I have seen a severe UTI mimic a stroke. It is serious.

Ongoing UTIs are hard to treat but made easier when the patient cooperates by drinking plenty of water. Once there is a tendency towards a UTI, it becomes an ongoing issue. It could be that the infection never truly leaves the elderly one's system. With one friend's mom, her behavior would change, indicating a UTI every time.

A sedentary tendency overcomes many elderly. If there is limited movement, there are still many exercises one can do from a wheelchair. If there is limited energy, there is nap time or iron supplements. Physical therapy can truly help to learn how to stimulate safe but effective movement. If their energy level is low, ask their doctor about which vitamin supplements are best for them, given the medicine they are currently taking.

Mom had colon cancer surgery at 92 years old. The first day the physical therapist came to work with her, she bounded out of bed. The physical therapist said to me, "I had rather have twenty over 80 year olds than five under 70 year olds. The under 70 year olds complain and whine about how much pain they are in. The over 80 year olds know that if they do not get out of bed, they will die."

Keeping a regimen of exercise is important, with whatever they are able to do, several times a day.

After one of my dad's surgeries, he was given exercises he could do while holding onto the kitchen counter. Three times a day, he and occasionally Mom, would stand at the counter, like a ballerina at the balance barre, doing his knee bends. They also used stand-alone pedals, like a bike, that sit in front of a chair.

This is necessary for health and balance as we are aging. Keeping some form of exercise, beyond getting out of bed in the morning, is vitally important to staying out of bed or a wheelchair permanently. Even something as simple as leg and arm raises while sitting in a chair. It was important for Mom to keep her balance. I would often find her standing on one leg with her arms raised in the air.

There are hundreds of websites that illustrate a variety of elderly exercises, even some on YouTube™. All exercises can be modified according to ability. Staying active is important for the mind and body.

Please understand this. There is no cure for growing older. Health is something to be cultivated in some and will be allusive to others. Some things can be made better. Know what those things are and let go of the rest. Elderly health is a roller-coaster ride at best.

Finances

Thankfully, my parents and step-grandmother had sufficient savings to help them with their expenses. They were very frugal in their spending as they aged. And, though we joked about Dad's ability to squeeze a buck out of a penny, as their caregiver, I was thankful I did not also have to worry about their finances as some of my friends have had to do.

Overseeing finances was a gradual process. Fairly soon after I moved back home, Dad took me to the banks to add my signature to all their accounts. Everything else financially remained the same.

When it was time to pay the bills, Dad would sit at the kitchen table with Mom. His handwriting had long ago become illegible because of the tremors in his hands from Essential Tremor Movement Disorder. Dad would tear the bills and tell Mom what to write on the checks. Mom would write the check number on the bills and Dad would put the paid bills in the ziplock baggie in the kitchen drawer. It was a process.

After one of Dad's lengthy hospital stays, we were talking about their bills. I suggested I take the bills after they had paid them and enter them into Quicken™ personal accounting software. I also downloaded their credit cards and cleared bank transactions. When Dad was so ill the last couple of years, I took Dad's role at the table with Mom paying bills.

When Dad passed away, Mom paid the bills, until she became confused about what she needed to pay. Then I wrote out the checks and gave them to her to sign. I certainly could have signed the checks since I was on the account. BUT, I wanted her to continue to feel as if she still had some control over something.

Even though Mom had sat with Dad at the table, Mom became overwhelmed when Dad passed away, completely fearful that she would no longer have adequate finances for her living expenses. Her fear was completely unfounded but real none-the-less. When her savings came down to a level that I became uncomfortable with, my nephew and I took on some of the household bills, saving her money in case it was needed for nursing home care.

Anticipating what their financial needs would be was always a guessing game. Household repairs were the most neglected expense. For years, the air conditioner was on its way out. Each time the repair man came, I asked him to hold it together with duct tape and bailing wire. Every hot summer, I would hold my breath. The day we buried Mom, it breathed its last breath and had to be replaced. I personally believe Mom arrived in heaven and said, "If everyone could wait just a minute – I have something I've been wanting to do," and then proceeded to give that old air conditioner a swift kick.

Property

As they became older, we had to make sure it was a safe environment. My brother and I would periodically walk through their home to ensure all walking areas were free from stumble hazards.

During one of Dad's hospital stays, it was possible he would be coming home in a wheelchair. I had the carpet ripped up and the hardwood floors refinished. I wanted movement to be easy so we also remodeled the bathroom to have a walk-in shower. We added grab bars by the toilet and in the shower, along with a shower stool and an adjustable handheld shower head. It became a fun family project of mudding and painting with my younger brother and his family.

When Mom fell one day after climbing a stool, we decided to get a home alarm system that included an alarm pendant to wear around her neck. Falling off the stool at least caused her to try to remember to wear it.

Stability & Consistency

A consistent routine is best with the elderly, just as it is with young children. I set aside the same day of the week, every week, for doctor's appointments, shopping, hair appointments or other errands. All doctor's appointments were arranged for those days. Some days, Dad went in the morning and Mom in the afternoon.

Looking forward to getting out of the house, Mom learned to depend on that day and would have a list of what she wanted to get done. I set aside that day for them and did not schedule anything else that would interfere. It was consistent for both of us. Some weeks, an additional doctor day had to be added to our schedule because there were too many appointments needed for just one day.

Every week, I printed out the next two-week's calendar with meals and my out of town speaking schedule. They had a separate calendar they maintained with their appointments, which was also added to my work calendar, so that I could be available.

My sister-in-law did the same thing with her mom, which allowed her to work four days a week, instead of five days. It is 4.3 days every month of non-revenue generation for the caregiver. That revenue is never recovered but it is a day sacrificed to provide for our loved ones. It is more typically only one family member providing that day, with little understanding from other family members of the income sacrifice.

Thankfully, my brother moved back to the area and could help with a day here and there. I have watched many of my friends having to take off work without pay, with no thanks from their siblings, if they had any siblings.

At this stage some elderly ones may feel they have become a burden to the caregiver and anyone who helps. They need to be reassured, sometimes often, that you are providing the same safety and security needs as you would to your family, because they are your family.

Love & Belonging: Friendship, Family, Intimacy, Connection & Companionship

My parents were fortunate in that they were connected to so many friends. They were very socially involved in younger years. As they grew older, the number of friends and social events declined. One night after the funeral of one of Mom's friends, she started crying saying she was going to outlive her friends.

Shortly afterward, I had her call seven other women to come over and play bridge. Social interaction is imperative. Isolation dulls their cognitive capacity and advances aging.

Touching and hugging my mom was important, especially after Dad died. Not everyone is a touchy feely person but Mom was one. She acquired hugs from everyone around.

One of the transitions I felt in becoming the parent was as her protector. She was, in so many ways, as innocent minded with her dementia as a child. My expectations of her as an adult had decreased because, quite frankly, she did not process conversations the same, often repeating herself.

She did process hurt feelings the same. She was just as tender-hearted as a two year old, and threw a few temper tantrums as a two year old as well. The more connected Mom and Dad were to others, the more they had a sense of purpose. The more isolated they were, the more they became depressed.

As Dad became less mobile, more dependent on others as well as his oxygen, he had less energy to be with others and, quite frankly, was less interested socially. Mom was always the more social of the two but I became concerned.

He would light up when people would stop by the house to say "hi". Those visits most often made his week, but then he would mope around the rest of the time, not moving far from his recliner.

Researching the issue, I discovered that depression and anorexia are common issues in the elder years. It was during the research I found some help with Dad's eating issues – sautéing the onions, for one.

Concerned about adding another medicine to his already long regimen, we never opted for an anti-depressant, and in fact, he was never consistently depressed. It was more of a situational depression.

My step-grandmother Chris did, however, get relief from her anti-depressant, when she would take it. Everyone got relief from her taking an antidepressant and everyone suffered when she would not take it.

Mom and Dad and I had many discussions about whether the time would come when they would be unable to live at home. It was less expensive to stay at home but more isolated. Most of their friends had moved to a senior living community just a few blocks away.

Even after Dad passed away, Mom was not ready to move to the senior living community. And, as long as I could be there, it was okay for her to stay at home. I was onsite, ready to remove the burnt pan from the stovetop if needed. It would have been a very different situation had I not lived on the property.

Intentional steps had to be taken so that they would still see their friends and live at home. We had friends over or I took them to visit their friends at the senior living community. I would take them to their church, arrange a ride or have the church bus come pick them up. Whatever they wanted.

When they remained social, they were happier, and ultimately, it was easier to take care of them. I kept remembering all the times one of them would shove me out of the house when I was young. As I became the parent, I was just as obnoxious trying to keep them involved as much as possible.

My goal was four to five socialization events a week. Church counted as one. Bridge as another, eating out with family or friends another, etc.

During the holidays, their home was the center of activity. We tried to have as many gatherings as possible. It was imperative for their sense of belonging. Regular phone calls to family that lived away helped and emails were fun for Mom, who engaged with her cousin in Washington often.

Love and Belonging is vitally important for your elderly and cannot be overlooked or overshadowed by providing organizational needs. Love and Belonging must be intentional, accentuated, highlighted, and emphasized. Love and Belonging is elementary to their sense of purpose.

Self-Esteem Needs: Confidence, Achievement, Respect for Others, Memory

The previous three needs can be provided for by the caregiver. These next two needs are dependent upon the first three being fulfilled but will be attained by the elderly one themselves. If the first three are not fulfilled, then there is no motivation to attain the next two needs, beginning with Self Esteem.

Confidence

When the body begins to age and fail, confidence wains. Walking becomes less assured with or without the aid of a walker. Breathing becomes difficult without mechanically supplied oxygen. In the event of a stroke, the body is uncooperative, while the mind may still be available, but perhaps not accessible.

Confidence wanes and embarrassment rises with the decline in being able to control bodily processes. So much of their purpose is questioned when there is a loss of mobility, function, social interactions, memories and income.

A lack of confidence can ensue if the elderly one moves to a different residence. A change in schedule will cause a lack of confidence. If anyone lacks confidence, they are unwilling to take certain risks. Their self-esteem plummets. It is a vicious cycle.

Mom would often give up trying to do something before knowing she truly could not do it, again, exhibiting a child-like behavior. I refused to rescue her because she could do so many things. She needed to remain independent for as long as she could.

Achievement

As they watch their hard-earned money dwindle, and they realize they have no means by which to earn more, this is a big change. They are at everyone's mercy where their money is spent. Living on such a fixed income is frightening.

If they feel they have failed in life, this becomes even more drastic. Regret is a dangerous thing, especially in the elderly. Guilt can be overwhelming and depressing.

Achievements become a different definition late in life, yet the heart still wants to achieve or conquer something.

My Dad has a junior high school named for him in Arlington. It was a major achievement, honor and milestone of his life. Nothing would ever equal or come close. A problem with high achievers in their elderly years is not achieving at the same rate or in such monumental ways in later years.

As often as possible, we would connect with this achievement by visiting the school, participating in school events or school parties. Again, social interaction is imperative. Principals, teachers and staff would often come to visit at their home.

It was hard for them to be confident and have any sense of achievement when they were incapable of accomplishing some of the smallest of fundamental tasks. We learned to focus on what could be accomplished.

We worked on large 300 piece puzzles, which helped motor skills as well as a sense of accomplishment. This was a much smaller puzzle than what they had worked on in earlier years, but still something they enjoyed. Reading or listening to audio books was another enjoyment they did not need to give up.

When Mom would resist a previously agreed to social function, I could tell confidence was not high. In bridge, she was afraid she would play the wrong cards and make her partner lose. She played hand bells well into her eighties for an older church hand bell group until her fear of playing the wrong notes overcame her.

They both enjoyed being outside so we built a patio where they could sit and enjoy the sunshine, when available and warm. I still needed Dad's help with the yard work, though the chores were aligned to what he could do that day.

Achievements for the elderly ones become daily goals, not as much lifelong goals as they had in the past. Three times a day exercise. Five times a week socializing. The word achievement took on a completely different definition for what it had meant previously.

Respect For Others

This was a tricky one. As they grow older, there is often no filter on what is said. They had a stronger perspective on what they wanted and when they wanted it, regardless of what anyone else was doing.

In the beginning as the roles were changing, it certainly felt they did not respect me. There was a lot of arguing. As time progressed, their respect deepened. They had never to that point had to rely on me in making the decisions. And their trust eventually prevailed.

Memory

As my business grew, I considered them my Board of Directors. Dad had owned his own business and Mom had a way of stating the obvious. I often told them about clients and asked for their input.

It is hard in the new-found role of being a parent to your parent, to watch your once vibrant and strong parent struggle with tasks, or to see their memory fail or to be the recipient of a tongue lashing, out of their frustration.

Self-esteem is fragile for anyone emotionally child-like but a significant danger is entering the elderly years with existing problems in their own self-confidence or self-worth. I have seen this happen with elderly women who were married to overbearing men who controlled their relationship. They grew old together then he died. She grew old but had no belief in her own self-worth or that she could accomplish the smallest of tasks, most often bill paying. Depression can ensue in these situations and may need caregiver intervention as well.

Self Actualization: Purpose, Expression, Spontaneity, Acceptance, Experience, Meaning & Inner Peace

Purpose

Mom asked almost daily after Dad died, "Why am I still here?" She had been with and cared for Dad almost 61 years and struggled to figure out what she was to do with all her spare time now, when she felt there was truly not much to do.

In the beginning, I created a **What to Do When You are Bored list.** We gathered note cards so she could write notes to her friends. We updated her address book so she could get her friend's phone numbers all in one place.

For a year, it was a struggle. Truly, after a year, she had figured some things out, but not without a lot of conversation. She became the person that called her friends to check on them. Many asked me at her funeral, "Who is going to call me now?" "I looked forward to her phone calls. Sometimes she was the only person I talked to all day."

Mom did something that helped her enjoy life and gave her a reason to be here. She did figure out her purpose in being alive.

The elderly need a means to express themselves. They need to know they are still important to others and have a purpose. If they have no purpose, they give up. They cease to be all that they were at one time or that they could have still been.

A sense of purpose is essential to health, a reason to persevere when health is declining. For some, it is seeing the grandkids grow up. For others, it may be to see a daughter get married. People are very typically relational; it is why they will get up in the morning. For Mom, she did not want to miss anything.

Expression

Their purpose will find expression, expressing themselves in whatever way they are capable of doing. Stories, stories and more stories - some stories you may have heard hundreds of times but expressing it to you, at that moment, may be relevant. Listen between the lines for that meaning.

As we age, whatever filters existed between the brain and the mouth diminishes. Mom said things I would have gotten my mouth washed out for in younger years. She told me she earned the right to say whatever she likes but I stated that I and everyone else had earned the right not to listen.

Uncanny, peculiar, never heard before words may be spoken by your elderly one so that you may do a double take to make sure it is truly them speaking. I often asked if she believed what she just said. Only a few times did I even attempt to correct because most often the correction was not worth the energy to argue when I knew a younger Mom would never had said what she had just said.

Spontaneity

Spontaneity is entirely a different being with the elderly and is dependent upon whether said spontaneity creates confusion. New experiences or unplanned activities can create confusion. Being spontaneous can conflict with an already established schedule if the elderly one has even slight dementia.

Mom did not enjoy much spontaneity for that reason but Dad totally enjoyed taking a detour from the established routine. The key is in knowing them and what they are capable of both mentally and physically, just as you would a child.

Meaning and Inner Peace

Meaning and Inner Peace sounds like a '70s term. I have seen such an extreme scale of inner peace in the elderly. As the mind is aging, the ability to acquire "an at peace feeling" is strained. I would interpret this to "is their heart at rest?" They have lived life and have now grown old. Are they content? Their cognitive reasoning can affect this peace.

During my childhood years, my neighbor was like a grandmom to me. She was the one I would go to when I was frustrated with parental issues. She was always at peace, with a calm soothing voice and a sweet chuckle.

Yet, dementia deteriorated her mind so that in her remaining days, she fretted about the end. She was not cognizant of what she was saying, as she tossed to and fro in the bed, repeating, "I'm so scared. I'm so scared. I'm so scared."

This was a woman of known peace and yet in the end, was not. I was fortunate that both parents were at peace to the end.

Sadly, my step-grandmother Chris was a different story. Most of the understanding I have of the negatives of caregiving, come from taking care of her. And, she was most certainly not at peace. This sounds harsh but I know there are others reading this that can relate. I was thankful to have Mom and Dad who were a counterbalance to Chris.

In Chris's situation, I did not become the parent. It was not a role change. It was a duty change. There is a difference.

Role changes happen to the extent the elderly person allows. I do believe it is built on trust, but in Chris's situation, however, all her relationships were built on a level of mistrust. It is from that level that she operated relationally.

Through the elderly years is typically when the Self-Actualization level occurs, not all elderly will work through the Hierarchy of Needs to the top of Self-Actualization. Most have come to know and accept their flaws and are at peace about it by the time they reach their elderly years. Some are very tenderhearted about it. Some just flat out do not care.

Taking a cue from Abraham Maslow, who incidentally passed away at 62 years old, focus on the positive qualities in your elderly person, not their shortcomings. If you accept the challenge of caregiving, there is a shift in your role in your future.

Chapter Five
Honesty: Ongoing Communications

Communication was an area I failed at with my siblings and, as a result, it made it my caregiving duties harder and my interactions with family members more strained.

After you have the initial conversations with your family about caregiving, you may be thinking that is all that is needed.

Oh, no. Not so.

The definition of communication according to Merriam Webster™ is:

- to give information about (something) to someone by speaking, writing, moving your hands, etc.

- to get someone to understand your thoughts or feelings

Communication is ongoing because the subject of the communication is still living and the need for ongoing communication is still necessary. Communication was great between my parents and me. But I did not communicate often enough with my siblings about what was really going on with our parents day to day, changes I was seeing, complications I anticipated, etc..

Communicating with my siblings the number of doctor's visits, the number of issues, the number of business interruptions, and the number of day to day issues with my siblings would have been helpful. It would have circumvented any potential thoughts our parents were supporting me.

After our parents were gone, of course, I realized I made it look easy because I busted my butt to be organized. I kept all the necessary time needed to attend my parent's needs documented in my electronic calendar. Should I had ever been asked, I could have easily printed a report with the details. It would have been far better for me to be honest in a monthly communique of some kind.

Communicating their finances would have helped as well. Every check one of my parents would write to me for a reimbursement of something, I would keep the receipt and write the check number. All my parent's finances were kept in Quicken™ personal accounting software so that I could produce a financial report at any given notice.

Communicating is a form of accountability. Healthy communication is imperative when caregiving. Unhealthy communication most often occurs when there is foundational a lack of healthy communication, resulting in hurtful comments, demeaning comments, and simply untrue comments.

After September 11th, 2001 as the stock market crashed and my young business was at a standstill, I considered dissolving the business to take a job offer. Consistent salary, benefits, and retirement were all very alluring. I KNEW the value I brought my parents by being onsite, which required a flexible job. Both parents were stable health wise and seemed to be doing well at that time, so working for someone else seemed a viable option.

It would, however, make me less available to them and would require them to hire someone to do what I had been doing, but my parents did not have those financial resources.

I had talked to them about my employment options but they were not very excited. One afternoon, Dad walked out to my house and asked if we could talk. We sat on my small porch and he asked me not to take the offer for two reasons. First, he believed in what I was building in my business and secondly, he wanted me to stay available for them, for what he could see for them ahead. It was a very serious conversation, discussing alternatives and options. He knew if I were to take the offer, I would be traveling, not at home or available.

My decision was easy. I committed to stay. He was scared of what the future held for him and Mom. I saw it in his face when he asked. I wanted to be there for both of them. I knew my business would eventually pick up, as it did.

Dad never told anyone about that conversation, even Mom as I found out later. I expected both of them to initiate a conversation with my siblings about all I was doing for them. But that never happened either. For me to do so, seemed like whining or complaining or tooting my own horn.

I am not sure why they did not. They gave the appearance that everything was okay, running smoothly. There was no indication as to the reason it was running smoothly - because I was taking care of a great many details of their everyday life.

So imagine my surprise when a family member suggested I should pay more than utilities but also rent for living in the guest house. They were unaware of what I did because it had never been communicated. In my efforts to cause my siblings no concern, some assumed I was freeloading off our parents.

Hindsight is always 20-20. Communicating monthly to everyone would have made them much more aware of what was being done. It is so much clearer now, with my own caregiving experience and listening to the stories of others, to understand communication is the number one challenge/issue in caregiving.

A friend told me her parents bought a house in another town three hours away, in the town where her brother lived. Her parents never even told her they were considering moving away. Her brother assumed their parents had talked to her about it and never mentioned they were even looking. She felt betrayed by all of them.

As she told me the story from over 15 years ago, the hurt crept back into her voice. She still felt betrayed. Never assume your parents have shared their intentions with all the family members.

Communication starts before it is needed and definitely before there is a crisis.

If your family does not currently have honest communication, that lack of communication does not get better without hard work. Lots of hard work. It will not heal itself.

What you avoid today gets worse tomorrow. If you have siblings, you need to spend time talking with your parents together. Yes, everyone's schedules are chaotic but make it happen. This is important.

When you are communicating with your parents, realize these are not the same parents who raised you. These parents are elderly, frailer, cannot see or hear or think as well and are frustrated they are aging, that their bodies are failing them. And, quite frankly, they grew up and matured just like you did, hopefully.

One on one communication with your parents needs to be consistent. If you are consistent, you will notice subtle changes sooner. Some friends that live a distance from their parents call them every morning on their drive to work. Some call the same time three to four times a week. Some call on the same day every week. Be consistent.

Communication Roadblocks

There can be roadblocks in communicating effectively with your elderly ones, such as:

Their ability to comprehend or to talk. Just because you think they do not understand or they cannot respond does not mean that you cease communicating with them. To do so is very demeaning to them. Treat them as though they can completely understand at all times, regardless of how frustrating it is to you. It is not about you – it is about them.

Family drama. A history of emotional entanglement, he said/she said, finger pointing blame game, not talking for years, buried anger/hurt/resentment makes it all difficult to carry on adult, emotionally mature, responsible conversations. Now is the time to put away the past and deal with the present. If you choose, it could also be a time to heal the past.

My schedule is more important. Remember when we thought technology would make communication easier? I actually think it has made clear, authentic communication more difficult and it is certainly made our schedules more chaotic. There is now less face-to-face time that keeps relationships honest. This chaos presents itself to others as your schedule is more important than others. If you are not the president of a country or the CEO of a Fortune 500 business, you can find a time to communicate. Even a CEO can find time to communicate. Schedule your communication if you need to do so but this is truly important to do with all of your family.

Texting is not a healthy form of communication because it can so easily be misinterpreted. "What did she mean by that text" happens all too often. Texting is often a cop out to a voice conversation. Pick up the phone and call.

Don't want to pry. Never shy away from a subject because you do not want to pry. Be bold but gentle. I had friends who never talked to their parents about what they wanted because they thought it would be prying. They did not pry right up until their parents passed away. After they were gone, there were many regrets in not knowing necessary details.

"I know better than you" mentality. Never interrupt anyone regardless of how important you think what you have to say is. Never criticize anyone regardless of how wrong you believe their thinking is. Never ever throw a tantrum and walk out of a conversation. You have to step up to the plate and be the adult, be the mature one, regardless of how you do not want to take the high road. You must listen to all the hearts involved, siblings and your elderly one, weed through all the emotions and practice effectively listening. If it gets out of control, practice deep breathing exercises to calm your soul.

Never assume someone feels or thinks a particular way until you have actually had a conversation with them. Assumptions are dangerous to effective communication. In the same regard, do not assume everyone knows how you feel regarding a particular topic unless you have had a very honest, direct communication with them about that specific topic. Do not beat around the bush. Get it out – do not make them pull it out of you. If you make them pull it out of you, you are manipulating the people and the events around you. Grow up.

Harsh personalities. Some people are just more harsh than others. Harsh people are often not well received. This I know well. Harshness is a form of defensiveness. I can still be very harsh if I feel the need to defend myself but have softened over the years and have learned there is a way to be direct without being harsh. People cringe with harshness and will not open their hearts.

Many families fall apart when their parents become elderly. The family may have begun unraveling long before but their aging parents then became a catalyst. The added pressure of caring for aging parents only makes a hard situation worse.

Communication Recommendations

For some reason, communication is often the hardest to do with your family, those humans you have known and lived with for a long time. And there is often a "sibling pecking order."

We grew up with a certain form of communication with our parents. I communicated with our parents differently than my brothers did. My sister communicated differently than us. The point is that we all have our own style of communication with the people that raised us. My parents and I joked with each other, were sarcastic with each other and stated our mind quite directly.

My sister often said that she could not believe I had said what I did in response to something they had said. That is because as kids, we would have been disciplined for that form of communication. But as adults, we were a bit more direct and honest. As my parents and I aged, our form of communication also aged, as our relationship moved from child and parent to adult and adult. You have to determine the best way to communicate with your parent as they age to elderly.

In order to avoid communication conflicts:

- Keep any emotions in check. Listen to each other without any accusation. Try to stick to the agenda without entangling emotions or worsening already entangled emotions.

- Always keep a sense of humor. Laugh with everyone about funny stories, but never at someone else's expense.

- Understand that emotions may be raw. If someone is more emotional, be understanding.

- Be an active listener. Do not figure out your answer when you should be listening. Repeat back what the other person said to clarify that is what they actually meant.

- Be patient. It may take your elderly loved one some time to say what they think or feel, especially if there are overpowering personalities in the room. Give them the freedom and the space to make their heart known. Wait for answers - be comfortable with no one talking, to give the elderly one time to answer.

- Speak clearly and slowly. Face the elderly one when talking - it makes it easier for them to understand, even if they are only slightly hard of hearing.

- If you say something you should not have, deal with it immediately. Apologize quickly. When dealing with elderly loved ones, you do not want to wait a very long time to apologize.

- Watch your tone, not everyone else's tone. You are not responsible for how anyone else communicates but yourself. Be a good example and always watch your communication tone.

- Let your actions speak louder than your words. It is a pet peeve of mine when someone says one thing but their actions scream another. If you say you will do something, follow through. If you say you love them, then act like it. Use endearing behavior and words.

Family Meetings

Somehow, good and honest communication must be made and made often with the entire family. With a lack of communication, people will draw their own conclusions based on their own perspectives. The stronger the lack of trust for the caregiver, whether warranted or not, the more communication is needed.

One way to communicate is through prearranged family meetings. A family meeting is beyond sharing a meal, visiting on vacation, or a day out shopping. A family meeting is planned. All family members must attend. If not everyone can make it to the meeting, Skype™ is a wonderful alternative. Due to the nature of the meeting, it is good to see each other's faces. There is an agenda – it is a business meeting- the business of caregiving.

The subject of any family meeting is about the elderly loved one(s), not about anyone else or sibling baggage or past arguments or how parents mistreated someone or any bitterness, etc. There is nothing about caregiving for loved ones that is about you. Ever.

A family meeting encourages shared responsibility. It encourages a team approach to caregiving responsibilities. The more it is treated as a structured business meeting, the more will be accomplished in developing the caregiving team but this meeting is not a medical care team meeting.

A care team meeting involves family plus doctors, nurses, etc. and develops a treatment or care plan for the elderly one. These care team meetings are typically held by the residential living homes, hospice or the hospital team.

The family meeting is just family. The first family meeting may be the hardest. Start at an agreed upon time in a comfortable place, perhaps in your parent's home or a park.

For the first initial meeting, invite only siblings and parents. Siblings can just be siblings without any undue influence of spouses. And, as in my case, should you still have a single sibling, it is most certainly more appropriate. After the initial meeting, as everyone agrees upon, include any other family members, friends or neighbors that will be helping in the caregiving responsibilities.

Try to schedule these family meetings on a regular basis, quarterly if needed. It is always better to start having family meetings when the elderly ones are not so old but still active and able to more fully participate. It is then a routine meeting discussing possible future needs and it will then be less overwhelming when the future does arrive.

Everyone will have their own agenda but encourage everyone to make a list of topics they feel should be discussed. This helps define what is important to each family member.

Take turns leading. It does not need to be the primary caregiver leading the meeting. In fact, it puts extra stress on them to do so. And, the same person is not to lead every meeting. That is not leading. It is an attempt to control.

Make sure everyone has a voice, especially the elderly one(s). When a subject becomes uncomfortable, soften the direction taken but do not argue. Arguing does not accomplish anything and often destroys any benefit gained. If the elder is not joining the conversation, ask them a question and wait for the answer to get them involved.

If there are existing family hostilities, consider having a neutral family member/friend/pastor/social worker lead the meeting, one that everyone agrees upon. People are often too enmeshed in their own feelings and agendas that you may need someone outside the family to lead the meeting.

Establish agreed upon ground rules. Here are some suggestions:

- Establish a time limit, not allowing one person to dominate the conversation.

- Speak one at a time with no interruptions.

- If the conversation becomes heated, take a ten minute break.

- Everyone is to tell the truth - dishonesty only sabotages future communications.

- Keep the conversation positive.

Have everyone put their cell phones in a basket, on mute, and then put the basket in a closet or in another room. Cell phones are a distraction and often give the appearance that whoever is on their phone (checking email, news, etc) is not fully engaged in the conversation. Have everyone check their phones for important messages every couple of hours but then the phones go back in the basket. Let everyone know ahead of time so that they can let their families know.

Appoint someone to take notes. Write down all the agreed upon tasks and who will perform them. Have the note taker create a document that will be emailed to everyone within a few days of the meeting. This is important so everyone remembers what was agreed upon and who is to follow-up, as well as when is the next meeting.

If there is someone who could not attend, make sure they get the notes from the meeting. Do not exclude them. Remember, the point is to increase communication, not to increase family division.

Family Meeting Agenda

What would a family meeting look like? If you need a little help getting going, use the outline below as a possible family meeting agenda. Of course, alter the agenda based on your particular situation. This is just to add clarity to a true family meeting.

Elderly One's Health Update
    How do they feel?
    Do they have any concerns?
    Doctor's Report(s)
    Any concerns over medications?

Living Arrangement Adjustments Needed
    Do they still feel safe where they are living?
    Is there anything that needs to be fixed?
    Are there any safety hazards that need work?
    Is it time to consider an alternate living situation?

Primary Caregiver's Report
    Summary since last meeting – any noticed changes
    Concerns
    Upcoming schedule conflicts
    Respite or help needed? Schedule it.

Caregiving Adjustments Needed
    Chores – meals, cleaning, laundry, doctor appointments
    Emotional support
    Any changes in documents

Financial Concerns
    Review income
    Review transactions
    Review savings
    Discuss any changes needed

Review Task List
    Topics to Discuss Next Meeting
    Schedule Next Meeting Date

Family Meeting Strategies

The following are a few suggestions that can help keep a meeting moving and will help accomplish goals faster and more efficiently:

- Remember the goal – to provide quality care for the elderly loved one.

- Have the meals during the meeting time catered or be pot luck. No food prep or cooking during the meeting. This makes it easier to focus on the agenda at hand.

- The first meeting may, quite frankly, be a disaster. Learn from what went wrong. Do not avoid a second meeting because the first, or any subsequent ones, went awry. Keep in mind the goal and check emotions at the door.

- Set the tone for open and honest sharing. Avoid the "I don't care" or "whatever" attitude. That is not being honest. Also avoid the opposite "it's my way or the highway" attitude. Be open to suggestions and compromise.

- If there is a lot of resistance, let everyone think about it. Do not push. It is unsettling for anyone to feel they are losing control, especially the one being cared for.

- Never ever do for your elderly what they can still do for themselves. They still need to feel they are in control of some things in their life. Do not take that away.

- Go at the loved one's pace. Get them talking and telling stories. Your agenda is to make sure their remaining days are lived out to the fullest and happiest they can be. Do not rush because you have somewhere else to be. Make them and your siblings feel they are the most important people that day to talk with.

- Everyone may not leave the meeting happy with the results but everyone is still needed and needs to be included.

- If you are not the caregiver and you have a suggestion, please be ready to take on that responsibility yourself, rather than adding it to the duties of the primary caregiver as that takes more time away from any personal or work time they may have in 24 hours.

- Do not be afraid to explore the "what-ifs" of possible future care. Ask the elderly loved one what they want should their health necessitate a change in their current situation.

- No decision is to be made without the elderly one's input. Treat their desires with respect, even if what they want is not possible. Even if you "think" they do not comprehend what is being said, get their input.

Family Meeting Questions

During the initial family meeting, you might need a little help knowing what questions to ask. There are four areas of responsibility. Here are a few additional questions to ask your family members and yourself.

To the recipient of caregiving:

- What does growing old look like to them?

- What do THEY want?

- What do THEY want you to do?

- How do they feel they are doing, honestly?

- Is there anything they are afraid of in growing older?

- Is there anything they need?

- How does the elderly person feel about their driving? Ride with them every chance you get to make sure they are still safe when driving. Be understanding. It is the reality of their losing independence.

- Do they feel safe where they are currently living? Is there anything that needs to be repaired or improved?

- How is their appetite? Have they noticed a change? Are they choosing healthy food to eat?

- How is their energy level? How much are they getting out and about?

- Have they battled any depression?

- Are they actively exercising?

- Do they feel cared for and loved?

- Have they noticed any decrease in mobility? How is their sense of balance?
- Do they have anything they want to say?

To you and your siblings?

- What do you see your role in caregiving being?
- Be realistic - what do you have to offer in time or finances or support?
- What do your siblings want to do?
- Who will be the team leader? The primary care provider?
- Is there anyone else that can help when it is needed? A neighbor? Another relative?
- What does the elderly one's future health look like?
- What does everyone understand the elderly loved one desires?
- Who is going to oversee their finances?
- Is there a current need to supplement their finances? Will there be a future need to supplement their finances?

If you are going to be the primary caregiver:

- Are you the most logical choice or a self-appointed choice?
- What are your motives? Chances are if you are reading this book, your motives are that you love your parent, regardless of any past or current conflicts. Make sure your motives are in the right place.
- Do you have a good support system? Family, friends, doctors, church – you will desperately need a group of "go-to" people.
- How much time per week can you commit? Understand what time is required now, becomes greater as they grow older and their health begins to decline. In other words, it may be a minimal requirement now but down the road, the time needed could easily multiply.

If you are NOT going to be the primary caregiver:

- How can you support the primary caregiver?

- What can you do in your life that will help them in theirs?

- Have you told them how much you appreciate the role they have taken on? Gratitude and appreciation need to occur on a regular basis. Send a card, flowers, a phone call, a gift card, or yourself so they can take a break.

Family Meeting Toolbox

www.mattersoftheheartcaregiving.com has documents to download to help gather information needed from your elderly one. Click on the Family Tool Box tab and enter the password "Iforget" to access.

Designing Your Long-Term Care Plan is a brief and informative article written by Kathy Dorsey, CLTC. It discusses options to consider when planning for the care one can receive when needed.

The **Document Checklist** provides a list of necessary documents, the date of their completion or newest revision and where the document is located. Items such as the will, medical power of attorney, healthcare directive, DNR (Do Not Resuscitate), health insurance policies, burial agreements, prenuptial agreements, adoption papers, home titles, and so many more. I wanted to make this as easy as possible for you to gather all the information you could at the family meeting about all these documents, with everyone present.

I asked my dad many times if he had shared or explained the will with the rest of the family. He emphatically said yes but had indeed not done so. It should have been brought up when we were all together, not discovered after he passed away.

The **Emergency Contact List** provides the names and best phone numbers for family members, friends, neighbors, hospital, church, attorney, etc. A one page sheet, there are additional spaces for you to use as needed.

With growing technology we now need a **Password List.** Banks, Credit Cards, the computer, email, house alarm codes, ATM codes and blanks for you to fill in. Needed are the websites addresses, login and passwords. It should go without saying that this checklist must be kept secure at all times, perhaps a bank lock box.

The **Prescription Checklist** we kept digitally and printed every time there was a prescription change. One was kept in our parent's wallet and/or purse and the local siblings also had a copy that we kept with us. This list states the prescribing physician, the official drug name, how many, how often, with food or milk and what it is for. We added the last column after getting so many questions from Mom about her medicine.

After filling out countless pages of medical forms, I created a Personal Medical Information Form with all the information listed. This rarely needed updating and as they became older, it was much more difficult for them to remember when their surgeries were or any illnesses they had or if they had any allergies.

These are the documents I have made available as of the writing of this book but I am certain more will be added with time.

Getting all this information gathered with everyone present is helpful. One person may remember something for the medical history form that no one else remembers. Everyone hears the same information, which therefore, helps everyone be on the same page. During the initial family meeting would be a fantastic starting point to get everything, and everyone, organized.

Having said all this, it may take a while to encourage a loved one to participate in the family meeting. Some are very private about their finances and do not want their children to know.

However, this is detrimental to their future care and a hardship on their children. It may take time, but keep the conversation and determination going. Be persistent. Again, it is better to begin these meetings while the elderly one can participate and explain their desires.

Post Family Meeting

Now, what about after the family meeting? How does the primary caregiver communicate the ongoing care of the elderly one?

In the age of technology, I suggest a weekly or monthly parental update via email. List all the events of that time period, the time it took out of your own schedule to accomplish said events, if you had to take off work for any of the tasks and the mileage or expenses incurred.

Do not whine, simply state the facts. It is not a draw for attention. Not a "look at what all I have had to sacrifice to care for our parents." It is, however, a simple statement of the facts to keep everyone up to date and to help them understand it is not as easy as it looks.

"I wanted to keep you abreast as to how our parent(s) is doing both physically and emotionally on a **weekly** or **monthly** basis. I also want to let you know what was necessary to provide from a caregiving standpoint."

After listing everything that happened during that time period, then say something positive. "All in all, other than aging, Mom is doing fine. Thanks for any help you can give – It is certainly appreciated!"

At the end of the update, make a "How you can help" list and list 3 to 4 ways they can concretely help. Be concise in your requests. If you want them to call their parent, ask them to call on a specific day. Ask them to put it on their calendar because that is their day to have a conversation with their parent.

A friend recently shared that her parent had an emergency trip to the hospital when a sibling was scheduled to come for a visit from out of state. The sibling canceled the trip because the parent was in the hospital, instead of coming to help. "It sounds like you have everything under control, so I'll come when she's better." That was not the response my friend wanted to hear as she was buried under work with project deadlines. She needed help with their mom even more while she was in the hospital. The sibling's response? "Mom is being provided for in the hospital. I cannot provide care for her there so I will just come at a later time."

The suggestion above regarding email updates was in response to our conversation. The sibling never considered that they would have to take off work to be available for doctors, do errands for the parent, care for the elderly one's residence, etc, while the parent was hospitalized.

Another friend said she might as well have been an only child because then there would be absolutely no expectation in ever having any help. Again, she made it look easy.

Send the updates even if the sibling says it is not necessary. Never sabotage yourself as a caregiver by not initiating communication. Never expect others to ask how they can help. Typically, they will not. Ask for help they can give but do not demand. Do not throw it back in their face when they do not help. It is hard not to but restraint is needed....often.

A private Facebook™ page can also be created for family. I know many that have this to share family news as well as caregiving information and needs. The updates could be added to this page, so it would never get lost in the email shuffle.

I have talked with many whose siblings do not help with their parents, but instead assume everything is under control. Because of that assumption, no one volunteers to provide relief care or respite care so that the caregiver can take a break.

Another aid in communication is a shared Google calendar. An online accessible amazing technical tool, why not use it? Put all the grocery runs, mileage, doctor's appointment, hospital trips, everything, on the calendar. Each sibling has their own color. When they participate with caregiving, they can put it on the calendar. This will also help let everyone know of upcoming events and appointments to aid in planning ahead or providing respite care.

What if your siblings will not participate in a family meeting?

Many friends have unparticipating siblings, who are unwilling to be available for a family meeting.

How can you still make them a part of the process?

As primary caregiver, I recommend you communicate with the unparticipating sibling to keep them informed via email or the private Facebook™ page.

You cannot change them. You cannot force them.

It may be they will eventually participate once informed. It may be they never participate in the care. But you will do your part by keeping them informed.

Communication is foundational to caring for your loved ones. Communicating with your siblings, your extended family, the doctors, and other care providers – it is absolutely essential and will make their remaining years as peaceful as possible.

Perhaps the transition after the parents are gone will be peaceful as well.

Chapter Six
Heartache: Empathy vs. Martyrdom

Caring is often made more difficult by the one being cared for.

My dad's mom passed away when he was 13. Long after she died, my granddad robbed the cradle and married a young gal six months younger than his only son. My step-grandmom, Chris never had children of her own, with her first husband (my granddad) or the other two husbands she outlived.

Chris loved football, more specifically, she loved Cowboys football. She could name all the players. She loved Troy Aikman and was truly concerned about all his concussions. She did have some sense of empathy, albeit for someone she had never met.

Chris had a green thumb with anything she grew. Both her front and back yards were a gorgeous bouquet of roses, irises, cannas, and many other colorful flowers. She would spend hours pulling weeds, trimming the bushes and cutting the dead flowers. She could seriously bring a dead plant back to a beautiful flowering bush!

When I was young, I enjoyed many pleasant hours with her in the yard but I lost that Chris years later. She still worked in the yard and garden but her words did not match the beauty in what she grew. Her relationships, in fact, cultivated the opposite of that beauty.

I saw a distinctive aging change in her between her second and third husband, and even more marked after her third husband passed. I saw a somewhat seedier and greedier side of her that I had never seen before as a child. I saw manipulation, control, and dishonesty up close and personal.

Dad said Chris had always been that way but it was easier to mask when she was younger. She was overly sweet to those she thought would do something for her. And if she was disappointed, she made it known. Whatever filters she had originally ceased to exist.

I made a mental note in regards to Chris – whatever bad characteristics you have when you are younger, those same characteristics are way worse when you get older. That should frighten some of you. That should also frighten some of your children!

Her third husband passed after I had moved home to care for Mom and Dad. I started visiting Chris more often, taking her places as she had never gotten her driver's license. She was completely dependent upon getting a ride or taking the bus where she wanted to go. She still lived in the home my granddad built, in a nearby town. I felt compassion for her because I also never had kids and desperately wanted her to know I was there for her.

Enter the third elderly person to caregive. She was selfish, strong willed, angry, bitter, shrewd and conniving. She was haughty with her family because we were the least likely to be manipulated but sweet and endearing to those she could manipulate. She would lie, if she needed to, to get whatever she wanted. The list could become quite long of those bad characteristics that were now fully engaged in her elderly years.

I made sure everything was organized and taken care of with Mom and Dad because Chris was an added responsibility. I did not have help with the three elderly ones until my nephew moved back to the area. All other family members were geographically unavailable. It was truly up to me.

There was a time I should have walked away from Chris. In fact, there were many times I should have walked away from Chris, but I kept trying. Some friends called it a misplaced sense of responsibility but if I did not take care of her, there were no other family members geographically close to do so. Family is supposed to caregive, right?

It was with her that I determined I wanted to be a blessing to those around me when I am old, not a curse. I want loved ones to be eager to come see me, not come see me because it is their responsibility or that they feel obligated.

Some days, I wanted to bash my head into the wall. Mom and Dad could be slightly argumentative with me at times but both of them together were not as stubborn as Chris. She would dig her heels in on a completely illogical decision that could be detrimental to her health or safety.

There was a constant war between empathy and martyrdom that battled inside of me when I cared for her. I was completely empathetic when I started but then when she became difficult, a real challenge to care for, I became a martyr because I was trapped into caring for her.

Chris had a very non-trusting, superstitious nature, with a sixth grade education. I think that limited her cognitive abilities greatly when she was younger, much less when she became elderly, and it most certainly defined what she thought was appropriate socially. She was not dumb, by any means, but she made decisions from a limited scope of understanding.

Sadly, by the time she passed away, I was relieved. I had lost my true relationship with her years prior and I had become simply someone who did things for her.

Where is the line between empathy and martyrdom - to care for someone because you truly empathize with the need versus because there is no one else to do the job? Since she never had any children, Chris feared not having anyone to care for her in her elderly years. It is one of the reasons I have long term care insurance now.

Before, during and after every visit with her, I tried to put myself in her shoes. After being beat up emotionally with each visit, this became harder to do. During her hospital visits, she was demanding of my time, that I had to be there. She would spend hours telling me stories of how horrible my granddad had been to her, and, of course, how great of a wife she had been to him.

After one such visit, I remember coming home in tears. It was really hard to understand why anyone would want to taint what few memories I had of the granddad I adored. My dad's response to the stories was to "consider the source."

I could not protect her from herself and her ongoing unwise decisions. Her decision making power should have been relinquished years before I had the first power of attorney.

The first time I became power of attorney was after she broke her hip. She needed help to pay her bills and oversee her medical care. We had actually been to the attorney the previous year to talk about a power of attorney before it was needed and the attorney talked her out of it saying that "the family can steal from you."

Though most certainly a true sentence, I always have to wonder about the perspective of one to make such a statement in front of someone they do not know, who is indirectly the one they are talking about. When Chris broke her hip, the process of getting power of attorney was mandatory to oversee what she needed. Good thing she was still able to give consent.

I kept all her financial records in Quicken™ personal finance software. She understood nothing of computer software and was always asking questions, suspicious I was stealing money. I showed her all the bank statements and the checks to assure her I was trustworthy. There was strong accountability but truly her minimal education kept her from understanding or trusting any of it.

When she decided she had had enough of the rehab center and demanded to go home, she called a friend to come get her, then revoked my power of attorney because she "wanted to do whatever she wanted to do without my nose in it."

A few years later, she was in the hospital a second time. She begged me to come visit immediately, that it was urgent. She was afraid someone would steal from her while she was in the hospital.

Before I agreed to be the power of attorney the second time, I had a very honest and direct conversation with her. I explained there would be no third power of attorney, that this was it. If she revoked the second power of attorney, I would not do it again. I made her repeat what I had said to ensure that she did completely understand.

Dad tried to talk me out of doing it the second time but I did it. Again, I was empathetic to her situation - she had no children to fall back on to help her. It seemed the right thing to do.

Over the next year and a half, she argued with everything I felt should be done to help her live in a safe environment. The house was not safe because of her roommate. The roommate was her longtime next door neighbor who had hoarded so much that she could no longer live in her own home. Then, you guessed it, she started keeping her hoarded mess in Chris's home.

Four times Chris called wanting me to evict her roommate. Three times I went through the process and would get to the end and she would call to say never mind. One time, I went through the information with the roommate, giving her notice to move, only to have Chris, the next day, tell her roommate that I was trying to get rid of her, that she did not really want her to go.

In a year and a half, I moved again from being empathetic to completely feeling like a martyr. Chris never said thank you, I am sorry, or acted in any helpful way for her own care.

She revoked my second power of attorney the day before my dad, her "step-son", died, and I received the attorney's letter of notice the day after he died. The timing of her revocation was stunning. In a millisecond, I severed any sense of responsibility or protection. I was all done. I no longer felt empathetic nor a martyr.

The revocation of her power of attorney was completely intentional, with every ounce of jealousy, haughtiness, and cruel intent. She did not even come to his funeral. She wanted the focus to be on her and her importance, over my dad. That was never going to happen, nor should it.

I no longer needed to believe I should continue to put myself in a place to care for her. She chose her caregivers. This time, she revoked my caregiving and chose another non-family member caregiver. So I was done. She chose a "gold digger," lurking in the wings, to become her caregiver.

She attracted the less successful people in life (addicts, alcoholics, prisoners, etc.,) with her "contributions," I think because she could be the dominant person, the smartest person in the room. They were in turn, attracted to her money. One of the ones who "befriended" Chris was the nurse of her cardiologist. She became power of attorney number three and the benefactor of the sale of Chris's home, antiques and half of the inheritance.

Beware – gold diggers are real.

There was even an Elvis impersonator who visited her nursing home that flirted with her. He tried to get her to put him in her will or make him beneficiary of her life insurance policy.

I was concerned about her money being stolen but her protection was no longer my job. I could walk away because she had chosen someone else to take care of her. I would never have felt free to do so without that choice. From a safe distance, I did ensure she had shelter, food, clothing and provision.

I did visit, probably out of nursing home guilt, knowing there are those who never get visits from family. Mom would go with me – it was better in twos, a buffer.

I was called many times by her well-meaning friends to become her power of attorney a third time. She had asked them to call, thinking they would be able to persuade me. There was to be no third time, as I had told her. My boundaries had been set. I still had Mom to care for and a business to build.

All in all, there were four power of attorneys. I was the first and second power of attorney. There were two more after me. When she did not get what she wanted in manipulation, she would revoke that person's power of attorney and find someone else she could manipulate with promises of inheritance.

It never dawned on me that she had promised something similar to me when I took on responsibilities as the second power of attorney. "You are in the will and all the bank accounts have you as benefactor." It had apparently become part of her mantra.

Being allowed to only do what the elderly one allows you to do, obstructs your caregiving, or giving care that is needed beyond that allowance. Sometimes those restrictions are very real and very frustrating.

There are things in my life I know neither of my parents would have wanted me to give up, had they been able to make those decisions thirty years prior. I used to say, "a younger Dad would have had a different request" or "a younger Mom would have wanted me to take that job offer."

I know many people who have given up different aspects of their own lives to care for their elderly parents. Time needed to be spent elsewhere (work) is what is given up the most.

Twenty years before we are truly needed to caregive, things look very differently. I knew my parents wanted me to build my business. Yet, every time I went out of town to speak, Mom guilted me by saying, "I am sure when I die, you will be out of town speaking somewhere and will not be able to get back."

Twenty years before then, Mom would not have cared and would have told me to just live my life. The dependency on the caregiver changes their perspective on the caregiver's life and the time spent with them. It is never enough time.

Many sacrifice careers and potential retirement funds to care for their parents. Do those parents completely understand what has been given up? No, not at all. Would those parents have agreed to that level of sacrifice twenty years prior, when they had the cognitive reasoning to help with the decision? No, not at all. Yet we do.

A loved one would never fully understand the daily sacrifice that would be required in the future because we have no idea what the future will look like. As an elderly one, they are typically cognitively unable to process that sacrifice. Nor would they ever fully understand that the caregiver would still do it all over again, to walk with them during their last years here.

After Dad passed away, Mom and I had an understanding. I am not a nurse. I had no desire to take care of my mom's bodily functions, change any potential diapers, should she become unable to care for herself.

For me, I wanted to do everything possible to preserve the dignity of my parents. I felt it was a dignity issue to intentionally NOT be there when they changed my dad's catheter, or anything to do with any private parts. I felt the same with Mom.

They were, after all, my parents. We had indeed switched roles. I did not, however, want to assume all aspects of parenting, like bathing or changing diapers. Mom knew that and completely agreed. Many of you have not had that option and have had to become involved in very awkward personal care moments. I was thankful we never really had to make that decision.

Mom also knew that should her care surpass my job or the time it would take increase beyond what I could give, that we would need to figure out a different plan for her care. We would need to get help or move her to a full care residence.

In 2003, my 24 old nephew, my youngest brother's son, accepted a position at the local university and moved back. He had graduated from college, worked at another university and had two other opportunities at different universities. When he called to talk to me about the opportunity at the University of Texas at Arlington, less than two miles from where we lived, he told me that he decided I needed help with Nana and Papa, so he was taking that position.

I cried so hard after I got off the phone. He will never know the relief I felt for the added reinforcements. I was battle weary, worn out and exhausted. I felt like the soldiers at the Alamo, hearing that relief was on its way. I was in a daily battle that was beginning to feel a little overwhelming.

Why did he help? We had a great relationship to begin with. When he moved back, he was the same age as I was when he was born and we were fairly inseparable during those growing up years, while I was in college. I would "bail" him out of daycare and we would go play.

He was now bailing me out.

We immediately divided and conquered the duties. He took on ordering their medicine, picking it up and distributing the pills to their daily pillboxes. We figured out the meals together, he made the shopping list and bought the groceries. He also cooked the meals.

I had everything else: Mom and Dad, all their appointments, errands, social visits, house repairs, yard work, hospital visits, funerals, etc. My nephew was more than just a day to day help, though. He was beyond the tasks as he listened, sometimes daily, to my frustrations.

He was my sounding board and became, as we joked, my caregiver-in-training. During all their hospital stays, he listened to the doctors alongside me to make sure I did not miss anything they had said or had forgotten anything that needed to be asked. And, he made sure I was taken care of in the midst of everything. I am still thankful as I am not sure what those years would have been without him.

My youngest brother and his wife, moved back to Arlington the end of 2005, and again, I was so thankful for the additional help I received. He became the one to take our Dad to his doctor's appointments. This was a much needed break and felt like the cavalry had indeed arrived.

Empathy vs. Martyrdom

Empathy means the identification of feelings, thoughts, or attitudes of another.

Martyrdom means the sufferings (or death) of a martyr, a person who endures suffering on behalf of a cause.

My empathy led to martyrdom on many occasions through my caregiving years. I was not good at setting healthy boundaries, to protect myself and my future, and my elderly ones were magnificent at pushing those boundaries.

Henry Cloud, a well-known clinical psychologist, states, "We change our behavior when the pain of staying the same becomes greater than the pain of changing."[1]   I had read Dr. Cloud's book on boundaries many times, even prior to caregiving. His information came in handy.

Setting personal boundaries is essential to protecting ourselves and guarding our hearts.   Boundaries protect all our relationships and establishing boundaries helps us stay focused on what needs to be accomplished.

Setting a healthy boundary meant knowing and understanding what I could and could not do at that moment and for the future, and having the courage to do or not do it. Setting a healthy boundary also helps separate the needs of the one giving the care vs. the needs of the one getting the care.

Sometimes it is hard to distinguish between the two.   Lives become emotionally and physically enmeshed. That is not healthy for the caregiver.

When I would begin feeling like a martyr, I heard Dr. Phil in my head – "How's that working for you, Susan?" At times, I would just unload on a friend, mostly about Chris. At times, I felt she was my designated thorn in the flesh.

Those were the times I realized I could not take care of her any longer. That was not caring with empathy but caring with martyrdom.

Good or bad, I traveled often for my business as a speaker. I often left a day earlier than needed because I had to have a buffer day to get my head in to what I was to speak on, especially if it had been a rough week of doctors' visits or hospital stays.

When I felt overwhelmed with caregiving responsibilities, I would take a few days off, often to the beach. Just the seven hour drive of quietness to the beach was therapeutic. Having distance often provided healthy perspective in why I was overwhelmed and what needed to change, because quite frankly, it was not working out so great for me.

The reality is not all elderly ones are loving.

Some are flat out abusive.

Some lash out with unfiltered words.

Some never ever consider thank you being in their vocabulary.

Some cannot see past their own frustration with aging, their own ailments, to care how you are doing.

Because some elderly loved ones are completely miserable, they think you should be miserable too and do their best to make it happen.

That is where the boundaries come in. They must be enforced. When cognitive reasoning has diminished, the boundaries will always be one sided. You will need to be the one to establish those boundaries and stick to them. Here are a few enforceable boundaries:

- Thank goodness for caller identification. We cannot physically answer the phone every time it rings and get other things accomplished for the day. We hate to not answer because it could be an emergency. If it was an emergency, a message would be left. Set limits to retain sanity. Do it because you need the boundary, not because you are punishing the elderly one.

- Never put your life on hold. I began building a business in the midst of the caregiving. In the beginning, I still did things independently of my parents and my family, which is a healthy autonomy. It was harder in the end but sanity requires it!

- Your relationship with your family must always have priority. The relationship with your spouse and children will outlive your elderly parent. Your children will see the loving care you give to your elderly one as a model for how you want to be cared for in your elder years. Your family must have priority in the midst of consistent care for your elderly one.

- If your elderly one is in a nursing home, set the time you have to visit but do not be obvious you are watching the clock. Make them feel you chose to be with them for that time. And that they are valuable. Put the cellphone away. Every visit you could hear the same story over and over. It is okay – act like it is the first time.

- Any time your elderly one acts out in anger, it is time to leave. You must remain healthy mentally, emotionally and physically throughout the caregiving process, because you have no idea how long it will last. Preserve yourself! This is not being selfish. It is actually being very loving towards everyone else in your life. You are no good to anyone if you have been beaten down and have no reserves.

Mom went through a phase of anger and lashing out. One day, I went to the house to check on them both. She was not nice so I told her I was leaving but would be back in an hour to see if she could be nice. In an hour, she was still not nice, so I told her I would be back in two hours but if she did not choose to be nice then, that I would not be back the remainder of the day. We could try again tomorrow.

It was a little behavior modification for the elderly. She was a little nicer two hours later but begrudgingly so. It was actually a bit comical to see her try to be nice. I had to do this for a few days before it sunk in that if she was not nice to me, that I would not visit. Mom was most often lashing out at me because my visits were never long enough but once she saw that what she did actually decreased the time I spent with her, she started being nice. Depending on your elderly one's attitude before the aging process, this may or may not work, but it would be worth a try.

Behavior changes are most associated as a form of dementia. When I was growing up, it was just called, "old age" or "hardening of the arteries." They have less perspective as to what is or is not appropriate behavior.

At many points in caregiving, I felt I was over the edge. At one of those points, a friend recommended a book by Richard Swenson, called **Margin**.[2] The Amazon book description states, "This book is for anyone who yearns for relief from the pressure of overload. Reevaluate your priorities, determine the value of rest and simplicity in your life and see where your identity really comes from."

As a kid, I wrote to the edge of the paper. Now in life, I had found myself living to and on the edge. It was actually a cathartic relief to know that I was not the only one that felt they were living life on the edge.

I read a good many books during the caregiving days. I have listed some of these in the back of this book. I would seek the books that would encourage me, maybe provide me an answer or two or three. At the time of my caregiving years, there was so little material on caregiving, so I would pick the issue I was feeling, find a book that addressed it, then apply it to my situation.

Some elderly are consistently verbally abusive. Maybe they were that way before they became elderly. Maybe it is their inability to function cognitively that causes a lack of filters on what they say. Maybe it is out of their frustration at growing older.

Whatever the reason, you must decide how to handle it emotionally. Maybe deciding not to continue in caregiving is the best option. If it is affecting your health, then you must consider that option. You should never ever be trapped into caregiving.

Counseling helps. Caregiving support groups help. If you do not have one locally, start one.

Chapter Seven
Frustration: Patience Is Truly A Virtue

Patience is the capacity to accept or tolerate delay, trouble, or suffering without getting angry or upset. Frustration is the annoyance felt by being unable to do something, like be patient. There are many things that will frustrate you in your caregiving duties.

It is most frustrating to stand by and watch your elderly one grow older and weaker. There is nothing you can do to prevent the aging process and it can be entirely frustrating, for the one growing older and for the spectator/ caregiver. Let's talk about a few of the areas that cause great frustration in caregiving. Again, not that you can do anything about all of them, but I found learning about the objects of my frustration actually awarded me patience.

Frustration with Hearing Loss

My patience began being tested when Mom and Dad's hearing began waning. Mom's hearing loss was significant.

At first, I thought they simply were not paying attention. Typically, Mom would ask a question then ask to repeat the answer. And to repeat it again. And to repeat it again. That many times, I was convinced she was simply not paying attention.

Mom had hearing aids beginning in her late 70s. Dad had hearing aids in his mid-80s mostly because if Mom had lost her hearing, she was convinced he had as well.

It was not because she was not paying attention, she truly did not understand what I was saying. Thus began a process of learning to face the person with the hearing loss and answer the question.

It was a process of learning to ask to be seated in a corner at the restaurant so that the person with the hearing loss would not have noise behind them, but only a wall.

It was a process of learning to speak clearly, not mumble. It makes me laugh now as I remember Mom saying, "Honey, you are truly loud enough. I simply do not understand what you are saying."

It was a process of eliminating additional noise. Having a serious conversation with either of them in a crowded or loud room maximized all our frustrations.

It was a process of adapting. We learned as we went along what could be done to help them hear more clearly and we implemented whatever we could.

Several visits to the audiologist taught me that in age related hearing loss, it is the tones that are most often lost, not the volume. A very layman explanation: there are tiny hairs in the cochlea of our ear that send different sounds/tones to our brain that translate into words. The loss of these tiny hairs is erratic which causes us to understand one tone better than another, some words easier than others.

Different tones make up different words. Some who lose hearing, cannot hear the high tones in words. Some cannot hear the low tones that make up words. That is often why Mom understood half of what was being said - she could hear the low tone words but could not understand the high tone words.

Some people do not project well when they speak. The words do not make it far past their lips, as if their tone drops. Some people mumble, which is really difficult for a hard of hearing person to understand. Some people's voices are simply quiet.

Television volumes are often turned up, to the distress of everyone else in the room, because the one that cannot hear, cannot understand what is being said, not because it is not loud enough.

To remedy the volume issue, I bought a wireless speaker that sat between their recliners. The placement of the speaker nearby their ears helped.

Turning on the televisions captions can also help with regularly scheduled television shows, where the script is basically put on the caption at the bottom of the viewing area. Captions can cause some confusion if it is a news report, where the dialogue is being inputted at the same time it is being said. Those captions are not always accurate and, with an already decreased cognitive capability, it may cause some confusion.

The gym where I work out has televisions to view on each of the cardio machines. The captions are available to read for the newscasts but the sentences are often left incomplete or skipped altogether so that the news makes no sense at all. I can only imagine what it would be like with a decreased cognitive ability.

Consonants are the hardest to understand and a noisy room makes it more difficult to understand annunciations. Requesting a corner table truly helps with the noise control in a restaurant, the one with hearing issues sitting with their back to the wall.

When dealing with hearing loss, always make sure there are no other issues, such as a wax build up. It sounds gross but it is an issue. Their primary care physician can determine if this is a problem and provide the remedy.

Knowledge is our friend! After the audiologist visits, I better understood hearing loss which gave me more patience. Mom told me that she understood me better than others, probably because I was around the most, but she also learned to read my lips. Since I would most often stand in front of her to speak, it apparently helped significantly.

The most frustrating time for hearing loss was the "I'm heading out the door and you are asking a question" times. I would have to close the door and walk back to where she was physically to answer because she never would have heard my answer otherwise. It was as if she forgot she would not hear the answer as she asked the question, so I had to remember she would not hear the answer and go to her to answer.

Speaking louder is typically an offset of not being able to hear adequately. Mom's hearing loss was much more significant than Dad's. They both spoke louder when they did not have their hearing aids in, which was always a clue to me they had taken them out. Dad would take his out (or turn them off) when he was tired of listening to Mom.

They both had to learn to whisper all over again due to their hearing loss. In the quiet settings, such as a church service or a funeral, their voice would sound out as they would "whisper" something to me. I could never respond because they would not have heard a whisper! Knowledge was a great thing because once we discussed it, they would both try to "whisper" to me more quietly. Laughs always ensued when whispers were still loud.

Bodily function noises (aka belching) also became louder because the one with the noise had no idea how loud they had become. Those times required gentle intervention.

Some of the funniest times were after I lost some of my own hearing. That made for some completely misunderstood conversations that most often ended up in laughter, with Mom and I both having limited hearing.

I was in downtown Atlanta, on the top floor of the Omni Hotel in 2008, when the top of a tornado ripped through me and the hotel room. With not a scratch on me, the intensity and noise of the tornado took 26% of my right ear's ability to hear and created nerve damage for the left ear. It also created havoc on some internal issues. But when the barometric pressure changes, I am more reliable than the weatherman, as the pressure builds in my inner ear like a hot poker!

When a tornado hit south Arlington close to noon one day, I knew at 10am that something was changing in the atmosphere. I had shooting pain driving me to my knees through my left ear, as if it would explode. Some people feel it through their knees and backs, but I feel it in my ears. Mom gained quite a bit of grace after I experienced my own hearing loss.

We were fortunate to have a great audiologist, not just someone who wanted to sell them the greatest and best in hearing aids. There are plenty of those audiologists in every town.

A great audiologist spends time, testing and making sure there are no other issues causing the hearing loss. Then when it is necessary to fit with hearing aids, their recommendations are not based on profit but what is the most reasonable option for their elderly budget.

Frustration with Natural Aging

Taking Mom to the grocery store became an exercise in patience. I could never take her if I was short on time. One learned if they were going to take her to the grocery store they must have an open schedule. She read every label, on every can, sometimes twice. Because the cognitive reasoning had been diminished, it took longer for her to process what she had just read. A short stop by the grocery store would be over an hour.

True to Mom, it never failed that she would get to the checkout and remember something she had forgotten. It scares me now when I do the same thing.

Patience is letting go of that we have no control over. She truly was not trying to test my patience. She just did it so naturally!

Because cognitive abilities are diminished, the processing of what is read takes longer. Thus, shopping experiences take time. We also saw this with watching new television shows or movies.

I would have to pause what we were watching to make sure she understood or heard. She loved to watch MASH, Matlock, Perry Mason, or Murder She Wrote because she remembered the characters and understood what was predictably going to happen.

Frustration with Dementia

Dementia is truly frustrating but it is absolutely not what anyone would ever choose for themselves. In fact, most people fear getting any form of dementia. As with old age itself, there is no cure.

The most obvious symptom of dementia is memory loss.

It was Sunday afternoon and my youngest brother and sister-in-law had just left. Mom stated they were sure dressed up. Did I know where they were going?

They had just left church and came by our house on the way home. She had been sitting there when they explained where they had been and that they were going home but hearing it from them did not help the information attach in her memory.

After they left, she asked every 10 minutes, six times, the same question, using the exact same words, the exact same tone, with absolutely no recognition that it had been previously asked. I was curious but she could be easily offended. I had to ask gently. After the sixth time of asking the same question, I said softly, "Mom. Do not take this personally because I am just curious. I am intrigued with how the brain works. Do you have any recollection of asking that question before?"

She was immediately defensive but then saw I was truly curious. I explained it was like her brain was starting a circle with the question but could not quite complete the circle with the answer. There was a definite disconnect and I wanted to know if any of it sounded familiar as she stated it again for the sixth time.

I truly was curious, which feeds my desire to analyze everything. How in the world can our brain make such a distinction as to have each question phrased exactly the same, even to when she breathed between questions? I even started phrasing my answers differently, engaging her in conversation about the answers, wondering if that would help. Nope.

When I asked after the sixth question and we discussed the brain and the dementia, she never asked that question again. It was very intriguing.

Dementia alters behavior. I have never had to study it. I lived with it.

We had a friend of mine over for dinner one night. Mom and my nephew had a fight and she was not coming to the table as long as he was in the house. She was completely acting out as a two year old.

After thirty minutes of her temper tantrum, part of it in front of my friend, I went over to the recliner she was sitting in and spoke quietly close to her face. "Mom, if you are going to act like a two year old then I will give you the options of a two year old. You may go to your room until you can return and join us civilly. Or, you can come to the table now and have dinner but you must behave as an adult, not a two year old."

I figured she would stomp to the bedroom and slam the door but she eventually came to the table and was pleasant, though not talking to her grandson at all.

Dementia is an overall term for memory loss and other brain dysfunctions that affect day to day life, with many different possible types of dementia. Dementia can also be drastically affected by a major illness; any major surgery, cancer, heart attacks, chronic obstructive pulmonary disease (COPD), and many more.

One of Mom's friends had knee surgery, which resulted in having Multi-Infarct Dementia, also known as Vascular Dementia, most often caused by surgery. Her behavior changes were severe and drastic and long term.

While she was in the hospital, Mom, Dad and I visited many times. She had no clue who we were and, at one point, asked her daughter to tell "those people" to leave. It was heart breaking but that was our first glimpse at how dementia works. She did end up recovering some but continued to have ongoing memory issues.

Mom was diagnosed with colon cancer at the age of 91. Colon cancer is not merciful but it was a hard decision whether she would have surgery. High blood pressure was a chronic problem. In fact, her high pressure was normal for her. Though it was possible she could have a stroke during surgery, we did opt for surgery after getting the okay from her cardiologist.

It was not without its drawbacks. Mom's dementia had been somewhat mild up to that point. Not so after anesthesia and surgery. We also began learning with Mom that pain meds take longer to process out of the body with an elderly person than a younger person. Normal dosage often does not consider an elderly body.

One morning after her surgery, my brother was chairside to her hospital bed. She rolled over and asked him, "I wonder what my Mom is doing right now. Let's call her." My stunned brother chuckled and replied, "Your mom isn't doing much of anything right now." We both figured she was talking about me but it rattled him to have her less cognizant.

After Dad died, Mom's dementia worsened, which affected her behavior. We visited the neurologist and he prescribed a medicated patch designed for dementia. It took a few months to see a difference.

After a couple of years, she wanted to stop the patch because she could not tell a difference. "It does not matter if you can tell a difference or not. We are not going to risk any changes." Or my sanity. I and my family believe that patch helped mellow out Mom, helping her with memory. After the patch, there was never another outburst or memory issue as drastic as those two stories .

Just as with her hearing loss, I focused on the dementia being the problem, not my mom. **Separating the disease from the person takes discipline.** Learning about the disease helped the process because I began to learn and understand it was a physical disease, not anything that Mom could truly control. That gave me much more patience and compassion to handle all the outbursts.

Frustration with Alzheimer's

While I was editing this book, a friend whose mom is battling Alzheimer's posted the following on her Facebook™ page. It shows the raw emotion of watching your loved one battle Alzheimer's.

> *"For those of us that this directly affects, we know it is so much bigger than your loved one not remembering who you are. It's an absolutely horrible monster of a disease. My mother was my best friend, the person who listened to me when I needed someone to talk to, my protector even when I was old enough to protect myself. This mother no longer exists.*
>
> *My mother now is usually the same loving mother I have always known, although there have been times in the last few years where she could be very hateful. My mother now asks me to come and get her and bring her to live with me. Unfortunately, this is not an option for our family. My mother now does not remember how to hold a pen and sign her name or what silverware is for. She eats with her hands.*
>
> *My mother now thinks my grown girls are back in elementary school. My mother now sometimes forgets my dad is no longer with us and wants to know where he is. My mother now doesn't remember that I just saw her yesterday or talked to her last night. To her it's been months. My mother now does not remember how to use a phone or anyone's phone number. The staff at the NH call me for her. My mother now thinks there are spies watching her and nothing I say calms her.*

Alzheimer's/Dementia robs not only the person with the disease but their family and friends also. It's like losing someone you love over and over sometimes for years. I miss my mother more than anything else in this world yet she is still with us, just a different version of herself! I hope this doesn't offend anyone. We all need a cure for this horrible disease!!"

Alzheimer's is the most well-known and severe form of dementia. Alzheimer's can happen at any age, but primarily the elderly. The loved one often remains physically healthy while the brain itself deteriorates. My mom's brother and her cousin both had Alzheimer's.

My uncle was happy and lived in a different world altogether. There were very few symptoms of his Alzheimer's until his wife passed away. He had memory loss but there was nothing more than mild dementia. As soon as his wife passed, the onset was drastic and severe. He passed from having mild dementia to not knowing his children or grandchildren in a matter of weeks.

Physically, he looked in great condition. He lost his hearing during World War II but other than that, he was an able bodied man. Looks were deceiving.

It was interesting how the parts of his real life meshed with the fantasy parts. Being analytical, of course, I tried to figure it out. There was absolutely no reasoning to his alternate reality. His brain only recalled that he sold real estate. Not that he was ever married or ever had children.

My mom's cousin's Alzheimer's took on a different dimension and it happened over a significant length of time. She did not speak or interact with anyone. She mumbled and stumbled around aimlessly. The brain had deteriorated in being able to communicate or recognize but her body was still healthy.

My mom and her cousin were raised as sisters, living in the same town. Many times an Alzheimer's patient will recognize someone from their childhood. They will remember stories and connect faces. My mom was hopeful but quickly broken hearted as her beloved cousin showed no recognition and had no speaking ability.

Another friend's dad had Alzheimer's. One of his first symptoms was ordering random things on the internet with his credit cards. It became an obsession for which the credit cards were removed from his possession. Another's mom made many random donations to random organizations that had sent donation appeals in the mail or that she had received an email from.

Though science has made great headway in the study of Alzheimer's, there is no cure. All of those that I have known to care for one with Alzheimer's, did so at home until it was no longer a safe option, sometimes being unsafe for the caregiver themselves.

To better understand Alzheimer's, go to www.AboutAlz.org. There is helpful information and videos in understanding the disease and its effects. One of the videos gives a great understanding of exactly how Alzheimer's works. Alzheimer's affects one in ten people over the age of 65. It starts in the part of the brain where memories are first created. An incurable disease, it can last eight to ten years. Knowing more about Alzheimer's may decrease your frustration, and increase your patience.

There are seven stages of Alzheimer's.[1]

Stage 1 shows no symptoms or memory issues.

Stage 2 shows minor memory issues but still undetectable by doctors or loved ones.

Stage 3 shows memory and cognitive issues. Doctors are able to detect impaired cognitive function.

Stage 4 shows obvious symptoms of Alzheimer's, having problems with simple math, recalling life histories, poor short term memory, and unable to manage finances.

Stage 5 shows a need for daily assistance, significant confusion, forget their own phone number, difficulty dressing.

Stage 6 needs constant supervision becoming confused in their surroundings, personality changes, bathing assistance, bladder and bowel control loss, and wandering.

Stage 7 is near death, losing the ability to respond to anyone.

There is no reasoning with an Alzheimer's patient. It only causes greater frustration and pain to try. You live in their world. They do not live in anyone else's world but their own. Nor can they. It is not by their choice.

A friend whose mom has stage 6 Alzheimer's has learned to say, "I will check into it," when her mom's imaginary stories are stated as real. She always plays along with any imaginary story, not trying to correct her mom that it is untrue.

Correcting their stories does not work but tends to only confuse them. What they stated, they believe to be true. If they have Alzheimer's, it will not matter how many times you correct them, it still does not change the truth they believe to be their world.

My friend belongs to a private Alzheimer's Support Facebook™ page for patients, caregivers, advocates, family, and professionals who need a place to vent, find encouragement, comfort and ask for help. It is an online support group with over 13,000 members. She said she rarely posts but just reading everyone else's posts helps her realize she is not alone.

When her mom had to be moved to assisted living, my friend made a Memory Board that wrapped her mom's room. The pictures were in chronological order with dates beneath and a list of the names and relationships of those in the pictures. This helped avoid questions that her mom could no longer answer, saving her embarrassment with the nursing home staff or visitors as well. I think it was comforting to my friend as well. Seeing pictures of her mom in younger years, reminded her of the relationship they once had.

Another friend's dad lived in an Alzheimer unit, while her mom lived off site. Her dad found a girlfriend, which hurt the family, but in his world, he did not remember being married, regardless of the number of times that his wife visited.

As Alzheimer's progresses, it becomes more difficult to live at home. A dear friend is caring for his wife with Alzheimer's at home. I have watched it rob him of his health. He hires "sitters" while he runs errands but they are finally moving to a place that will provide help in caring for her and give him much needed rest.

There is also often a violent, hateful side to Alzheimer's. With Alzheimer's, it is an expected, very real stage of the progressing disease. An Alzheimer's patient can also escalate when they are out of their normal routine or normal environment and can become confused as to what is going on, like at the hospital.

One friend's mom is in a locked home for Alzheimer's patients. The hurt was still obvious in my friend's eyes as she recounted to me things her mom yelled at her during this stage. She learned to separate her mom from the disease but it still wounded her heart.

There will NEVER be an option as nice as their homestead for an already fading memory and the transition in moving is a difficult one. Moving them sooner to a memory care residence, rather than later, helps them to adjust and get to know the community they will be living in before the difficult days ahead of memory loss.

An Alzheimer's patient's physical look may change over time and yet they are the same loved one you knew. Their voice may change as well but it is still the same one heard all these years. The memories will fade, recognition may stop and the frustration grows but they are still your elderly loved one.

The caregiver is often at a loss as to know how to patiently handle the changing loved one. Patience most often must be chosen. It is not something that will come naturally in the frustration of the many moments ahead. Patience must be chosen, put on and worn.

Dementia in any form is a true cognitive disease, for which there is no cure. Alzheimer's is fatal. There is not a time frame associated with the disease. I have known patients that have lasted less than a year and those that have lasted several years. The bigger frustration and heartache comes when they no longer recognize you. Nothing I could say would ever prepare you for that moment.

I asked the friend that shared her Facebook™ post to send me a list of six things she wished she had known before caring for her mom with Alzheimer's. She wanted to share these thoughts:

- Learn when not to take no for an answer. You know who your loved one is better than anyone and what works and what does not work. Example: When your elderly loved one is taken to the ER, the ER staff insists on evaluating them before letting any family go back. A person with Alzheimer's may tell the hospital they have fallen, when they are actually there for something entirely different. Be adamant about going back to their emergency room, to make sure they understand your loved one has Alzheimer's.

- Be prepared for the hurtful angry person your loved one can and will become. As hard as it is to do, you cannot take this behavior personally.

- Alzheimer's is much more than your loved one not remembering who you are. This particular memory loss normally occurs much later with the progression of the disease.

- It is never too early to evaluate your loved one's finances or assets. You need to know how much money there is in case your elderly one needs continuing care. It is expensive to be in a memory care unit and preparing ahead of time helps.

- Live in your loved one's reality, whatever that is in any given moment. The things your loved one describes or says happened, really did in their world. You must learn to associate with their reality as your own without correcting them in theirs.

- If they become obsessed with a particular topic, redirection is the key. With Alzheimer's, often one becomes obsessed with a particular story. Redirect to anything else - something outside, something you saw that day, a funny memory.

Frustration with Doctors & Hospitals:

What Is The End Desired Result?

There always seemed to be too much time spent on many doctors' visits. Actually, too much time spent in doctors' waiting rooms as well. And why?

In the end, the only real ailment my parents had was growing older. All the issues were related, beginning with "because of old age..."

Dad had chronic obstructive pulmonary disease from smoking until he was 65 years old, then his kidneys began to fail. He was on oxygen and a catheter for a few years, actually doing quite well, until he broke his hip.

Mom had high blood pressure and dementia, but other than that, she was doing amazingly well. She could sit in a chair, pull her leg up to her chest, and tie her shoe, never losing balance. I seriously thought she would live until she was 100 and still feel a bit ripped off that she did not make it to celebrate with Willard Scott on NBC.

I began going with them to their doctor appointments when they would come home with two different reports from the same doctor visit and neither was correct. What I had a hard time understanding was the number of doctor appointments that were required for the prescriptions. It was if they expected to cure old age.

I was the patient advocate for Mom, Dad and Chris. I hired and fired doctors. As they became older, one doctor consistently required a monthly office visit of Mom, with lab work prior to every other visit. All he did was use a stethoscope to check her heart, his fingers to check her pulse, had her say "Ah" and charged her for the visit.

His waiting room was full of elderly patients and one of their kids who had to take off work for the same routine. It was an assembly line of patient rooms, with the doctor in and out within five minutes. He was always late.

Beyond frustrated one appointment, I explained to the front desk I had three elderly ones to take to all their doctors' appointments and all the doctors made me wait. I told them I tended to the house, the meals, the yard, their finances, their lives AND I worked. I tallied how much time I had to wait, times the number of visits, times my hourly billable rate and told him that he owed me and I would be sending a bill.

That doctor was chronically late, even when it was the first appointment in the morning. His nurse told me he was never on time and it was not because of any emergency room visits. That was a blatant abuse of everyone else's time, so we changed doctors.

Another doctor also required visits every three months in order to renew prescriptions. During one of Mom's appointments, we discussed how purposeless the requirement was and he changed it to every six months, which seemed still too often but I relented.

Another doctor did not respect the family's requests. Another doctor's diagnosis was completely off base and after getting a second opinion, the family was glad we fired the doctor.

I advocated their best care often asking, **"If this were your dad or mom, what would you do?"** That question changed the course of treatment many times.

Though, ultimately there are many hats that you wear as a caregiver, first, you transition to become a Parent, and then you transition into a Patient Advocate.

I wrote symptoms down, even if one of my parents was embarrassed when I brought it up to the doctor, such as incontinence. I asked a lot of questions. I asked about each medicine's side effects to other medications. I clarified dosage amounts being suitable for elderly bodies.

As the body ages, our organs decrease in their functionality. It takes less fluid before a bathroom break is needed. It takes longer for our kidneys to process various medicines through our bodies, which can ultimately cause a buildup of those medicines in our system. Combine this with a decrease in metabolism (liver function) and physical activity, it can create a problem that we did not have before.

I saw this happen repeatedly with my parents, Chris and many of my parent's friends and friend's parents, primarily with anesthesia and pain killers.

When my dad broke his hip, the buildup of morphine in his systems caused further damage to his end stage kidney failure, suppressed his breathing with COPD, made him incapable of any therapy and, I believe, ultimately ended his life. I was out of town but my nephew and brother had to repeatedly request the nurses stop administering the morphine often, albeit as prescribed, because he was also hallucinating.

I personally consider morphine to be a dangerous drug to be used in elder care. A normal adult dose is not typically age considered and should be very closely monitored.

Mom had back pain for which she had several epidural shots. One flare up, the shots did not provide her any relief. The doctor prescribed her morphine for the pain. When she started hallucinating and became lethargic, I verified with the pharmacist the dosage. It was the same dosage given to anyone over 21 years of age.

Many friends have relayed the same information and feedback regarding morphine. If your elderly one begins to respond in an agitated or confused manner, consult the physician regarding the dosage.

To decrease frustration with doctors, consider the following:

- **HIPAA.** With new HIPAA laws, it is imperative for the primary caregiver to be given approval to speak to the doctor on behalf of the one being cared for. But, go one step further by also listing all siblings, an aunt, an uncle or a neighbor.

- **Never be the only one that can speak to the doctor.** There must be more than one person that is allowed to speak to the doctors or the caregiver will not ever get a break or will not have complete information because the doctors will have come and gone.

- **Do not ever be afraid to ask questions.** Keep a list if you might forget – that is what I did. Then take notes to communicate with others. One time, Mom was required to monitor her blood pressure three times daily. We had a clipboard with paper and drew columns. We took those papers in for her doctor appointments. We also wrote down anytime she felt light headed or had any abnormal symptoms. Often, the primary care doctor and her cardiologist would differ in opinion. My trust and respect was with her cardiologist so when her primary care doctor wanted to change the medicine her cardiologist had prescribed, I quickly questioned the move. He was surprised and truly could not give an answer for the change. I politely thanked him for his recommendation but said we will stick with the heart doctor's recommendation for blood pressure medicine. I did call the cardiologist's office to tell them what the primary doctor had suggested and received a resounding no.

- **Know the nursing shift changes and assess the ones you like.** Request the nurses that are committed to caring for your elderly one. Problems can get passed shift to shift. If it is a crisis time, make sure all the care team is on the same page.

- **Create a network of doctors for your elderly one.** This is important if there are doctors in your area to do so. Thankfully, we live in an area where there are options. Rural areas do not have the same options as we do. However, insurance companies have greatly decreased available network options.

- **Medicine Changes.** If there were ever any medicine changes, I had the changer of the medicine fax that information to the other doctors with an explanation as to why they felt the change was needed. My youngest brother had worked for a pharmaceutical company so any changes were also run by him. If he had questions, he would call the prescribing doctor. We also had a great pharmacist that we asked many questions.

- **Medicine Cost.** Some medicine became too expensive for my parents. In fact, they typically ran out of Medicare benefits in July, having to pay 100% of their medicine costs August through December. Mom wanted to quit taking all medicine. "I'm sorry. That is not an option." One year, their medicine costs were exorbitant. Living on a limited social security income, their medicine costs quickly consumed a majority of that income. I created a spreadsheet of all their medicine and dosage and faxed them to several area pharmacies. We decreased their medicine costs substantially by moving all their ongoing medicines to Sam's Club, without having to change their medicines. Any short term medicines, such an antibiotic, were filled closer to home since Sam's Club was farther away. Weekly trips to Sam's Club filled any medicine needs as well as medical supplies.

Beware of hospital visits during the holidays. We used to joke about how Mom would make a hospital run before Christmas because it happened several years in a row. It was not very funny, though. The hospital itself was typically short staffed so we had to be onsite to help more than normal.

We learned that most of the regular doctors Mom or Dad had seen before would be on vacation. The doctors on call were not familiar with their care.

They were often not full time doctors. I am sure some of the Doc Holidays, as we called them, were great doctors but one Doc Holiday was fired before we were tempted to physically throw him out of the hospital for his inappropriateness.

When I told their primary doctor, whom the substitute doctor was filling in for, what he had done, the doctor defended him, saying he filled in for him all the time, as if that was an excuse for his inappropriate behavior. We changed primary care doctors.

Mom and Dad's cardiologist was amazing. There were no excessive appointments and I honestly believe they lived as long as they did from his care. They were both in the hospital often. I knew what time he would be making rounds to his patients. If he walked into one of their rooms, and I was not there, he would ask where the boss was. I had his cell phone number, which he had given me directly for when Dad or Mom had a heart attack or a major issue. He also knew I would not abuse it. More importantly, I trusted his prognosis and his care.

My parents were both in intensive care quite a few times. One late night, the cardiologist and I sat at the nurse's station talking about his kids. He was human and cared about my parents. That is what you want in a doctor.

What was the purpose for the visit? As Mom and Dad grew into their 90's, it had better be a good reason to go to the doctor. It was hard getting the elderly out for a doctor visit and, quite frankly, it would have been better to go somewhere fun, like out to eat, than to the doctor for all those visits. Sometimes it honestly felt that all the doctor visits only created greater frustration for the caregiver.

What was the end desired result? My desire was to have my parents live out the remainder of their days as comfortable and as happy as possible. I truly wanted the best for Mom and Dad but they were not suddenly going to be any younger. There was and is no cure for old age.

"What is the end desired result in his care?" When Dad was in rehab for his broken hip, this question became more relevant than at other times. I wish it had articulated itself much sooner in my caregiving time.

After a prior hospital visit for which he was not expected to come home, I asked him if he wanted such heroic measures done the next time. It was a very serious conversation with Mom present. He said no, that the next time to just let him go. It was hard to hear but I had to respect his wishes. Having a Do Not Resuscitate document signed when they are lucid makes the process of saying no to extreme measures easier the next time around. I did not do so with Dad but thankfully did so with Mom.

When he was then in rehab with his hip and struggling a year later, I vividly remembered that conversation. He was in agony and rehab was honestly painful to watch. In one more consultation with his kidney doctor that my brother and I both respected, we decided to let Dad move to hospice.

Truly, my end desired result was to keep my parents from any pain and to keep them with me the remainder of my days. They were my family.

In caregiving, what is the end desired result?

For me, it was to have no regrets.

I reached a point that I realized they had lived a long time and deserved to have an extra scoop of ice cream at night if that is what they wanted. I reached a point with Dad that he could have anything he wanted. He had already lived past 90 years old and I did not think he would live much longer.

We had an agreement. As long as what he chose to eat/drink or not eat/drink did not cause adverse effects that would hospitalize him then he could eat/drink whatever he wanted.

Enjoy their remaining days. It is not necessary to argue. I gave in because it simply was not worth arguing and they wore me down. They are not children. Truly, it was their life. At that age, I just wanted them to be happy.

As a caregiver, that is a question you must answer for yourself. Your answer may be different but it demands to be answered honestly. **What is your end desired result?**

Frustration with Insurance Companies or Medicare

Every time you add or change a doctor, your elderly one must give new approval to the insurance company or Medicare for you and others to speak to them on your behalf. Often they require a document to be completed and faxed back.

With HIPAA laws to protect patient privacy, it has created a myriad of issues when caring for your elderly loved ones. The insurance companies must abide by those rules as well as doctors, hospitals, nurses - everyone who provides a form of healthcare to your elderly one or has healthcare knowledge regarding your elderly one must comply.

Keep a copy of your power of attorney or the form the insurance company provides on hand to fax back at their request. I must have faxed that form to Mom and Dad's Medicare supplemental insurance company a dozen times each.

Some of the medicine changes they went through were because the insurance company decided they were no longer going to provide coverage for that medicine, making that prescribed medicine an exorbitant luxury to those who were living on a fixed income.

It was frustrating because it was often not the best choice in care for the elderly one. Some medicines simply do not work with some people. The insurance company never budged beyond their initial decision so the elderly one was prescribed something else instead, simply because the insurance company would cover the less effective prescription.

This became a paramount issue when the drug the insurance company would cover conflicted with another drug they were already taking. Often two drugs then had to be changed, instead of just one.

It was frustrating because it took valuable time out of an already time short day to appeal to the insurance companies and converse with the doctors and often the pharmacists.

Frustration Leads to Feeling Trapped & Isolated

After Dad died, Mom's struggles with dementia were compounded by her true desire to know why she was still alive. She would ask me all the time – "Why am I still here?" After a few sarcastic answers, I would answer that I guess I still needed her in my life to teach me something. Or maybe her friends needed her to encourage them.

The bottom line was that if she was still alive, then she had purpose in living. She had to figure out what that meant for her.

After much conversation, she started sending cards and notes to friends, and calling them often, just to check in. She was her Sunday School's Sunshine Leader with updates on the sick or hospitalized. Most of her friends were like her – not driving and living at home or in a retirement community a mile away.

Those days of questioning her existence wore on me. Selfishly, the conflict rose in my heart every time I wondered if my life would ever be normal. Many friends quit trying to ask me to do things because it was too hard to leave. Mom did not require physical support but lots of emotional support.

The definition of frustration includes the prevention of a fulfillment of something.

My life was not the life of a normal 50 something year old. This was year thirteen of caregiving and I was getting pretty tired. I used to ride a bike, go to the gym, and camp. Now, I was lucky to make it through the list of to dos at the end of the day, juggling my growing business and Mom.

I quit dreaming about vacations and fun things I could do a long time ago. I could not plan anything because I never knew if I could actually follow through. I charged my cell phone every night and put all the phones by my bed in case I got a call in the night. I was on 24/7.

I was tired all the time, not having the energy to do anything. I am sure I was depressed. I had hundreds of friends and I was constantly with others but I was lonely. I felt trapped.

I needed an outlet.

My family has been Texas Rangers™ fans since they came to Arlington in 1972. I worked at the baseball stadium as a high school teenager the first three years they were here.

Baseball is the one sport that lasts most of the year. So, during all those long hospital stays, we watched baseball. Regardless of what was ailing them, they could track baseball. Pretty much nothing else on television sounded good but they would always ask, "is there a game on tonight?"

It seemed a natural progression that after Dad died, I wanted season tickets.

My nephew and I decided to buy seats tickets together and that became our refuge. We would leave for the ballpark with time to spare, as if we were going to work, and Mom would watch for us on television, with her Texas Rangers™ ball cap on.

The ballpark is the one place I could go, have a hotdog and a drink, and not think about anything except baseball. It quickly became my refuge from the stresses of caregiving. There are 81 home games every year. I bet we went to at least 65 home games that first year. It was the one sense of normalcy that I had and I clung to it. They were my outlet – win or lose.

There have to be outlets when you are the primary caregiver. One time, I wrote a list of all the things that made me feel good on separate slips of paper and put them in a jar. When I felt overwhelmed, I would pick one.

My favorite was a massage. Another was getting my car washed. Another was sitting outside in the sun. Another was taking a long hot soaking bath with a glass of wine, and nice bubbles or bath salts. Another was burying myself in a favorite fiction author. Another was going to the movie and buying popcorn.

I confess. There were more massage slips of paper in the jar than others. I tried to get a massage at least monthly and every time, my massage therapist would say, "Susan, you are so tight."

I loved to go camping, even if it was just one night at a nearby state park. Biking on trails was also a favorite activity. I had a friend that enjoyed doing both so I had someone who prodded me to do those activities with her.

Getting outside in the fresh air was important. As caregiving responsibilities increased, the activities I loved to do decreased.

Music had always been a part of my life but one of the most noticeable changes was my preference to quietness versus music while driving in the car. So, I began listening to more music without words, classical music, instrumental, or soft jazz.

I did learn how to be the queen of 20 minute naps. I would set my alarm for 20 minutes and tune out the world. It is a true discipline to tell all the things bouncing off the walls of your mind, to shut up and leave you alone.

Friends spontaneously calling to see if I could do dinner was easier than trying to plan ahead. Or to go shopping. Or to get coffee. To plan ahead required knowing how the day would go and I had no clue in advance. As a caregiver, you never know. I had broken too many plans to have the energy to plan ahead any longer.

Caregiving responsibilities gradually consumed my life. Friends eventually quit asking to do anything. If you are the friend of someone who is in the midst of caregiving, remember they may need to be more spontaneous. Do not quit asking. They want and need take a break.

By the end of my caregiving time, I was fairly isolated. I was attending Texas Ranger™ baseball games, but my time was primarily spent on my business or attending to Mom. There was not much time or energy left over.

Perhaps that is why I did not pursue getting out more often. I realized that whatever time I had remaining with her would be short.

It is also important your elderly one is not isolated and remains active.

After my nephew moved back, we built an outside patio for Mom and Dad to sit on in the afternoons. It was very simply made, with square concrete stones, cheap plastic chairs and a table from Home Depot™. They fell in love with being outside again and it became their rehab after hospital stays. They often drank coffee or ate lunch on the patio. One afternoon, Mom looked at Dad and exclaimed, "why didn't you build me a patio sooner?"

Sometimes we would load up in the car and take a drive to the lake, or to a neighboring town, or go see Christmas lights. Though still a bit isolated, it was a break in the monotony. It was just nice to get them and myself out. It was often hard to get everyone ready for the shortest jaunt but once we did it, we never regretted doing it.

Sometimes we would pack a picnic lunch. Fears of their falling kept us on paved paths but there were plenty of paved paths available.

Every time I suggested doing something, it met a lot of resistance. Dad had loved going to the junior high that bore his name. But, going late in his life, required a lot of preparation and a lot of energy.

Time to get ready always took longer than expected. Then, we had to add a rest time after getting ready. Sometimes it took two hours before we got in the car.

The older Dad got his resistance to going anywhere grew stronger. It would have been much easier to cave in and let him stay at home. But, instead, I coaxed him by using his own verbiage against him. "You are still vertical, so we are going."

They ALWAYS enjoyed being there once they got there. The exception to this, of course, was if they were not feeling well. I did not push then.

After Dad was gone, I challenged Mom to walk to the end of our long driveway or sidewalk twice a day, just to get out and be moving. Mom still played bridge with a group of gals every month and attended a senior group lunch monthly.

If you are able to do something fun with your elderly one, do it while they are able. When you spend time with them, you are reinforcing that they are still important to you, not a burden or just an item on the to-do list. You are creating memories that will return to you at the oddest times after they are gone and bring a smile to your face.

You can do something with your elderly one, even if they are unresponsive, lying in a nursing home bed. There is no way to know how much of their mind is trapped. Read to them. Play their favorite music. Give them a manicure. Rub their hands and feet with lotion.

You are showing love and helping them, and you, feel connected to the world, not isolated from it.

Here are a few suggestions of how to stay connected, not isolated:

- Keep a list of things to do that make you happy.

- Keep a list of things your elderly one can do to make them happy.

- Start a book club with your elderly one, a few of their friends and your friends.

- Host an afternoon tea or game time with elderly one and their friends.

- Bribe friends with pizza to help you paint a room of your elderly one's home.

- Check out Pinterest™ for ideas for projects.

- Go on a picnic to a nearby park.

- Interview your elderly one about their remembrances of historical events and video the interview.

- Play games. Something they have played before, nothing new.

- Do a puzzle together.

- Do stretching exercises together.

- Take lots of family photos.

- Go to a baseball game!

Final Word on Frustration

If you are a caregiver, being frustrated will happen but learning about the aging process can help. Planning ahead can help. Being prepared can help, but nothing will take frustration away all together.

If frustration builds up, it can affect you physically: make you sick, raise your blood pressure, cause headaches, chest pains, and shortness of breath.

A natural response to stress is to lack control in your own personal life. Some caregivers become alcoholics or smokers. For me, my frustration eventually shut me down from taking care of myself. I quit enjoying outdoor activities and quit working out.

Frustration can be dangerous. Take care of yourself first. You need to be in the best shape to take care of your elderly one. Frustration is the primary reason that one must keep their sense of humor in caregiving.

As a humorous side note, I asked my nephew what was the most important issue to include in this book. He quickly said, "Patience."

Then I asked, "What helped you with your patience?"

He said, "Nothing," and then laughed.

He is right. Most of the time, you just try to make it through without bashing your head in the nearest wall but patience is still something good to strive for.

Chapter Eight
Guilt & Resentment: Pendulum Swings

Though I moved before I needed to, I expected to eventually resent having to do so, especially as the years of caregiving drudged on longer than I expected.

I felt guilty. If I was not caregiving that meant both my parents would no longer be living. I knew I was "led" to take care of them but the negative feelings were overwhelming anyway.

When they attempted to guilt me, it provoked resentment that they were the ones I was caring for the most. When they acted entitled to my time and focus, it provoked resentment that it was never enough time spent with them. When they said something less than encouraging, flat out demeaning or hateful, I resented having moved home to care for anyone.

If I had a dollar for every time I wondered, "What was I thinking," I would be wealthy.

If you are reading this and you are not in a caregiving position, then you may think it is selfish of me to have felt this way. However, if you are reading this and you are caregiving, you get it. It is a fairly normal course of emotions.

My sixteen years of caregiving came at the most economically productive years of my life, from 39 years old through 55 years old - the time of life when most are really socking away for retirement, paying off the house, buying a new car, and occasionally enjoying a vacation.

Yes, I inherited a house. I inherited a house that needed many repairs and updates, that by the time I completed all of it, I could have bought a new home. I had to take out a mortgage for all the work that was done but the house my dad originally built is absolutely gorgeous. My retirement account has slowly been growing since my caregiving days are over.

Resentment is not limited to the caregiver. Resentment also involves the whole family. A friend has a young family and is responsible for a grandparent. "No one else would step up to the plate." With deceased parents, they went on to describe how they resented their siblings for not helping. Their siblings resented that they were expected to help care for the grandparent. The spouse resented everyone, including the grandparent for getting old.

What a mess. My friend said, "I feel badly for my grandparent. They didn't ask to get old and need help. I feel guilty that this has caused such an issue - guilty on all fronts."

And, there goes that pendulum swinging from resentment to guilt.

Another friend with a young family has cared for a grandparent, a mother-in-law, a father-in-law, and another grandparent over the span of fifteen years. All lived independent of my friend and her family, which caused for quite a bit of driving to provide care. Two had cancer. Two were just old. My friend is not a weak person but it was physically demanding and emotionally draining. Thankfully, she did not have them all at once.

It was a cooperative effort with her family and the kids pitched in with cooking and cleaning at their own home. The kids also spent time with a grandparent every Wednesday. Everyone had a responsibility.

To say one of the in-laws was difficult would have been an understatement. He also made poor decisions. Her father in law was harsh, bitter, mean and an alcoholic. He decided to turn off the hot water at his house, which meant his dishes were not clean. It also meant he did not bathe often.

There were many times his grandkids were not allowed to visit because of how he had treated them the visit prior. My friend's first responsibility was protecting and providing for her children, not her father-in-law. Often she had to provide care in spite of him. How he treated his family was something no one could fathom. They were there for him. It did not matter. Resentment rose with every necessary visit. There was never a civil visit.

I watched my normally easy going friend, through those years of her life, being beaten down and becoming emotionally exhausted. When her father-in-law did pass, it was sadly with relief.

What all of my caregiving friends have done is modeled how they would like to be cared for in their elderly years. Their kids are seeing them lovingly provide care to the elderly regardless of how they are treated but that is a difficult investment.

Guilt (n) "A feeling of responsibility or remorse for some offense, crime wrong, etc. whether real or imagined."

Guilt (v) "to cause to feel guilty (often followed by out or into)"
See also guilt-trip.[1]

That last part, guilt-trip, was Mom and Chris's recipe on a daily basis. They were the Queens of "Guilting" - ones who could make the subjects in their presence feel guilty about even the most meaningless things.

With Mom, it started early in my youth, through to her last days. She was good at it and cultivated it often. Most of the time, we would have a good laugh about her "guilting" attempts, since I jumped on every opportunity to point out their failure in making me feel guilty.

When Mom started "guilting" me with "I guess you will be gone on a trip out speaking somewhere when I die," she said she was kidding. I knew she really was not kidding. It probably scared her to think something could happen while I was gone. She depended on me.

There were times when I was made to feel guilty, when I had to enforce what I knew was the right thing to do.

I developed the phrase, **"I'm sorry but that is NOT an option."** This was a multi-use phrase that, unfortunately, I had to use often, for instance, when Dad wanted to leave his oxygen at home. He was embarrassed he needed it.

Try it on right now. Say it aloud as you read, "I'm sorry but that is NOT an option." Practice saying it void of any emotion, without any frustration, anger or dominance in your voice. State it as a fact.

There will be times when there is no other option to a decision that you must make. And, no matter how hard you try, they will never understand the decision. Remember, a diminished cognitive ability prevents reasoning to be involved.

They asked, "why?" a lot in the beginning but my reasoning was solid. After a decade, in response to the "Why," every now and then, I would throw in a "because I said so" and start laughing.

Because there was no handbook to caregiving and I was the first of my friends to journey down this road, I often second guessed myself, causing myself to feel guilty, with absolutely no basis for the guilt.

That is also normal. The pendulum swings between resentment and guilt are also normal.

Most adults would never say, "Oh, I hope I can be a burden to my kids when I get old and cause them to give up so much of their life." No matter how much time I spent with my parents or Chris, it was never enough.

Their activity had become limited and they were lonely and frustrated at getting old. Nothing I could have done would have ever taken away those feelings.

Being there more often did not work. Being there less often did not work. No matter what I did, I could not take away the real problem. There is no cure for old age. There is no fountain of youth.

I often had to choose between work (which equals money in the bank) versus some caregiving activity. My pendulum swung at rapid ascents and descents during those times. My clients were very understanding regarding needing to reschedule due to a parental crisis which happened, at times often. However, clients also pay for reliability. And, as an independent contractor, if I was not working with a client, I was not generating income to pay bills. There were no paid sick days or paid vacation days.

I was compiling evidence for prosecution of a substantial embezzlement case one Christmas holiday. I only took off Christmas day. Even then, my head was not participating in the family fun. Before and after the holiday, though the house was full of out of town family, I worked twelve to fourteen hour days, rationalizing the longer hours. There was plenty of family to oversee Mom.

What I did not know is that it would be Mom's last Christmas, that I missed out of all the fun memories of that holiday season. We do not know our expiration date and I falsely assumed Mom's was far away. This is the reason I will no longer work during the holidays. That is time I now set aside for my family.

Your pendulum can swing too and it is ok. Recognize it for what it is. If you feel the caregiving is overwhelming you, occasionally step aside. Ask for respite care from a sibling or check out a local assisted living community for respite care.

One of our local memory care facilities offers respite care by the hour. What a great offer for the caregiver. In fact, many of the retirement communities and assisted living homes offer respite care that can be used as a stepping stone to your elderly loved one moving to that residence. Especially when things are beyond your control and it is time to find an alternative to them living at home.

Making the decision to move your elderly one to a care facility is an emotional decision. Most caregivers will jump between moving and not moving multiple times. This process is a much easier decision if discussions regarding care facilities were approached prior to any significant need or any major decline in cognitive capabilities.

Realize the swings to guilt in the decision to move your elderly one to a care facility will be intense, and is often brought on by the elderly loved one. Resistance to change is strong and guilt can be their response, especially if they are afraid. It does not matter how logical the move may sound to you. It is emotional to them.

There are various stages and levels of care with various options. Let's look at an overview of each one with more detail following the overview. Prices are given on a national average.

Life alert system – living at home, this alert button can be worn around the neck, to be pushed in case of a fall or another medical emergency. It can be an independent monthly cost with a stand-alone device connected to the phone or internet, or it can be connected through the home's security system.

Home Health Care – a variety of options to provide care in their own home, such as housework meal prep, respite care, bathing assistance or companionship. Home health care costs vary depending on the services and the time needed, generally between $25-$35 per hour.

Senior Day Care Centers – suburban areas often have these centers available for the elderly one whose family works. Meals and activities can be provided and cost is up to $64 per day.

Retirement Communities – no supervision is provided. Small kitchens accompany a one or two bedroom apartment. There are many common areas with regularly planned activities and meals are provided. The apartments are purchased and owned by the elderly one.

Rehab – short term stays, most often after a surgery or illness requiring hospitalization, to gain strength or mobility or to retrain them for capabilities they have lost. After a hospital stay of at least 3 days, Medicare will pay for inpatient rehab for up to 100 days. The time clock starts when admitted to the hospital and ends after 60 days of not receiving any medical attention.

Assisted Living – for those with limited mobility issues and mostly independent living with some oversight assistance. Memory Care facilities are locked with additional staff. Cost is an average of $109 per day.

Acute Care – a continuation of hospital care but not at the hospital. This is most often covered by Medicare depending upon the nature of the admission. Costs vary.

Residential Care Home - in home living for a small group of adults. Meals, lodging and assistance with daily activities is typically available. Costs vary but are typically less than nursing home care.

Nursing Home – the staff provides full time care for the patient, providing medicine, hygiene, laundry service, meals, etc. Cost is an average of $229 per day.

Hospice – standalone facility or at home with trained staff for the patient and their family in the last days of the patient's life. This is covered 100% by Medicare although some prescription drugs may not be covered.

Life Alert Systems

After Dad passed away and Mom was home alone during the day, we talked about and decided to get a life/medical alert pendant on a necklace for her to wear. It was directly tied into the home security system for an additional fee.

It gave Mom, and me, peace of mind that if she fell, she would be able to get help quickly. When she did fall, she had forgotten to put it on that morning. She was a little leery to wear it after she accidentally pressed the button when she leaned against the washing machine, loading laundry. Because the pendant was connected to the alarm system, the police were dispatched and they kindly checked the house just to make sure she was safe.

There are many options available for life/medical alert systems. Some connect wirelessly, some connect through a telephone line, and some connect through the alarm system, such as ours did.

Some require a button to be pushed on the pendant. Some have built in technology that can sense a fall. Some have built in speakers in the pendant itself.

Some are waterproof, which is good since some are in pockets during a wash cycle. Some have GPS options. Some will alert if it is not being worn.

Some are month to month contracts, some are annual contracts and, beware, some are long term contracts and the costs vary for all. Evaluate your individual situation and decide what is best for you and your elderly one.

There are also electronic pill dispensing machines, so you do not have to worry about accidental overdose or not taking their meds at all.

Just as the medical alert systems, there are a variety of medication dispensers. Most are locked. Some will alarm when it is time for medicine to be taken, some have flashing lights. Some can dispense up to six times a day. Some will alert the caregiver if medicine is not taken from the machine. The medication dispenser was a great alternative for a friend's mom who was adamant about staying at home as long as she could, but always forgot to take her medicine. It is also a great resource for medicine control regardless of location.

Home Health Care Agencies

If your elderly one wants to continue living at home or simply cannot afford an alternative, and greater care becomes necessary, home health care agencies are less expensive than full time care in a residence home.

Home health care agencies can bridge a gap in care and provide companionship when you cannot be there. Having assistance is often necessary to prevent resentment from creeping in.

If your life demands attention in a variety of places, guilt in not spending time with your elderly one may be a constant battle. Sometimes taking care of their personal details takes time away from just spending it with them, enjoying them. Home health care can help most often with whatever you may need.

I often arranged visits by my parent's friends to take place while I was traveling out of town. Mom had one friend that would come pick her up for lunch when I was gone.

If your parent wants to remain independent at home, it is not a bad idea except when it is no longer safe for them to do so. Be aware your perception of "safe" will likely be very different than theirs. Always.

Moving To A Care Facility

The guilt we feel often allows them to stay at home long past the time that it is really safe. One friend was told by the Fire Department, after they had to come help transport the elderly one to the hospital that it was no longer safe for her to live at home. She had never been able to make that decision on her own because her mom did not want to leave. Every time my friend brought it up, her mom made her feel intense guilt for even suggesting she move elsewhere. However, when the Fire Department said it, that recommendation was final.

How do you combat that guilt? You may not be feeling guilt independent from the elderly one. Again, Mom was great at launching guilt in my direction. To combat the "guiltings," I would ask Mom and Dad questions:

- What are you afraid of?

- Why do you not want....?

- Do you trust me to make decisions?

- Would you not like to be the one to pick out an alternate living option?

- What would make you feel safe?

- What are your concerns in moving?

- Would you like a say in who you give your mementos to? How your belongings are dispersed?

Friends of my parents came over one day to tell them that they were selling their house and moving to a retirement home. Dad had a hard time understanding why they would do such a thing. They did not "need" to at that time as they were both healthy.

They moved to a high-rise senior living community complex, with one to two bed apartments. They had friends there so they would not be isolated. When they could no longer drive, there was a van that would take them wherever they needed to go. Meals were provided in dining rooms with various seating options and times, and the food was good!

They moved before they needed to move and, while they could still make that decision on their own, they started downsizing, before they needed to move. A friend's grandmom told me the same thing. She wanted to move while she still had a say in where she was moving.

Unfortunately, a larger percentage of elderly have to move to a greater skilled nursing care facility when they do need to move. It is often a result of an injury or illness. It is often in their minds a short term answer and they think will eventually be able to move back home, regardless of whether that is actually a viable option.

Retirement Communities are great first steps, being the first break from the home they were used to living in. Some retirement communities offer progressive levels of care, beginning with wholly independent living options through nursing home care. Some senior communities provide respite care should you need a break. It is a great "test the water" option while you are on vacation.

Independent Living is simply apartments where the residents are on their own. Home health care aids may attend them here but must be paid for privately or through their insurance.

Assisted Living is somewhat independent but the resident needs more oversight, than living on their own. Meals are provided but they must be mobile, perhaps with a walker. They must be able to dress, feed and toilet themselves.

Memory Care is essentially amped up Assisted Living. The staff to resident ratio is much higher and a greater level of care is provided. The cost will be greater as well.

Nursing Home Care provides full time hands on care with medical assistance, as well as daily living assistance. It is more labor intensive and much more expensive. Be prepared for sticker shock.

All nursing homes are not created equal. If your elderly one has impaired cognitive functioning, then narrowing down choices ahead of time would be a good idea. Dad went with me to find Chris a place to live the first time, after she broke her hip and could not live in her home.

We developed a game plan when looking for Chris's rehab, then again for a nursing residence afterwards. Here are some suggestions from that experience and a few from other friends as well. When you are checking out a prospective residence:

- Do not set an appointment prior to visitation. Visiting unannounced is key to seeing more than just what they want you to see. If you do not like the facility, then you are not wasting time with an appointment.

- Visit during lunch or dinner times. These are the times when the staff is assisting the entire facility at once. Make sure mealtimes are the least stressful as possible for your loved one – if they need assistance, is it available?

- Review the activity calendar and visit during those times to see if a) the activity is being held as stated and b) how many of the residents actually attend. Do they have activities which you and other family members are invited to attend, such as Valentine's Banquet, Super Bowl parties, etc.

- Call the facility to determine how long it takes them to personally respond to your call.

- Some facilities will be updated in the public places and present a very pretty picture. Look beyond the exterior. The staff is more important than the overall look of the facility.

- Ask about ALL the costs. There is typically a base fee, but what about additional charges: laundry, supplies, meal supplements, grooming, haircuts, etc. Read ALL the details of the contract agreement prior to signing. If there is vague language you do not understand, clarify with an attorney.

- If there is a facility doctor, make an appointment to ensure they agree to maintain any care or medicines that you feel are necessary. They should not override existing doctors.

- Do not pick out a home based on what you think they would have liked or based on how close it is to your home. Pick out their next place to live based on what they need today. And, if it is a little farther from where you live, then so be it. The elderly one's vote is important.

- Do the staff seem engaged with the patients or were they detached, on their cell phones, at the nursing stations? Were the residents left alone at tables, or wheeled up to the television with no companions?

I have never been in a nursing home that does not smell like urine. There. I said it. However, do not look at the place or base your decision on the smell, but rather the people who are there to care for them.

Obviously, I wanted a clean facility, with windows for plenty of natural light. They all have an odor. It will bother you the most, not your elderly one. The sense of smell also diminishes with age. It will stir up guilt in you in a heartbeat. Get over it and do not point out the odor.

Nursing homes are a financial investment for your loved one. If Medicaid or Medicare is involved, it becomes a tricky one. There are many resources available online to assist in figuring out the financial resources. One resource is a guide provided by Medicare[2].

It has a checklist to use when visiting potential nursing homes. The downside to the checklist is it was written as if the resident would have the cognitive reasoning to decide. This should never be a decision left up fully to the elderly one but they most certainly need to have input if they are able.

If your elderly one is resistant or even hostile about moving, getting their agreement does not always work. It was not a viable option for Chris to go home after she broke her hip. It had become unsafe for her to live at home any longer. After visiting a lot of assisted living residences, I found her a relatively new, beautiful place with a center courtyard full of roses. Her apartment had a beautiful view of that courtyard and it was clean and spacious.

And she hated it. She told all her friends that came to visit how much she hated it and that I was forcing her to live there.

And, I felt guilty. There was no alternative. She could no longer live at home. She did not tell her friends the truth of her circumstances and I resented her for the hatred shown towards me personally with her friends. From guilt to resentment is often a short distance.

After I moved Chris to her new home, the employees strongly suggested I not visit for two weeks. This was her adjustment period to acclimate to her new home. I would call Chris to check on her and when she would start yelling at me, I would end the call quickly, feeling both guilty and resentful.

Not all nursing homes make this suggestion. It is logical that the resident needs time to acclimate as much as possible to their surroundings, without depending upon a spouse or a child to do so. Calling to check on them is a great idea to let them know you did not just drop them off and forget about them.

One of the retirement homes was throwing a wine and cheese hour when I visited. They were having lots of fun socializing. That is now a requirement for me in the future!

What do you do if you suspect elderly abuse or neglect?

Recently a friend shared they suspected his mother of abusing his dad who had had a stroke. He was withdrawn but seemed to come alive when he went to adult day care. His dad winced when his mom would walk by. Remote cameras told the truth and they are in the process of moving his dad to assisted living and moving his mom to her own apartment.

Adult protective services is available to help those being abused by their caregivers. It is heartbreaking that there are those who will bully or hit your loved one in a home they believe is their shelter. If your loved one becomes withdrawn, you notice unexplained bruising, injuries or weight loss, or as simple as appearing not showered and/or wearing dirty clothes, pay attention.

Start visiting unannounced at their home or care facility. "Audit" the care the facility provides. Hang around at different times of the day and night. Then, if your concern is heightened by what you see, first report it to the facility's administrator, then report it to law enforcement. There are federal nursing home regulations that must be enforced, punishable as elder abuse or assault.

Elder abuse is sadly on the rise and must be reported. Do not merely think that it is your elderly one's dementia. Do your due diligence.

If you truly believe the care facility provides good care, the most preventable means against any elder abuse is to remain visible by visiting often and at various times of the day. Asking the staff questions lets them know you are paying attention. Also, take the staff treats every now and then. They are caring for your loved one and are members of your elderly one's care team. Let them know you care for them, as well.

I was fortunate that neither of my parents needed to move to a care facility. Just in case it was ever needed, we went beforehand to visit some of her friends in various nursing homes. When we would leave, Mom would say, "do not put me there if you need to put me somewhere."

When we left one care facility one day, she said, "I like that place. It's nice. You can put me there if you need to one day." It helped to know what she wanted but it was never needed. Those conversations with Mom removed any potential future guilt.

Hospice

Picking out a hospice is a little different. You know going in that they are not coming out. It is brutally hard on the emotions: overwhelming sadness and sometimes guilt.

Buckle up. It is time for the roller coaster ride of emotions to begin with the "what-ifs."

Hospice Care can be provided at home. It is most often not full time around-the-clock care, such as in a Hospice Facility. Mom really wanted Dad to come home to die. Because she was 92, that was not a good idea. I knew she would not sleep and that she would long remember that he died at home. She would never rest if he was at home, putting her own health at risk.

She was mad that my brother and I made the decision on a stand-alone hospice facility instead, but when Dad went into crisis that evening after moving him, she was truly glad we had not moved him home. Anything can happen in those last days. It ended up being such a positive experience, that Mom requested a hospice facility should she ever need one.

The more their wishes are communicated, the less we will question the decisions we must make. Ask them what they want before those decisions must be made. Mom made our decision easy regarding hospice by letting us know. Again, it is best of all of this is written and signed by the elderly loved one before it is ever needed.

Guilt guilt guilt

My guilt induced roller coaster ride included zero gravity drops: at not visiting as much, not staying long, taking a trip, not including them on events, etc.

Guilt does not require logic. For instance, it was rare I took an extended vacation in those 16 years. Five to six days was typically the longest.

I was petrified by the "what-ifs." What if I were gone any longer or if it was further than a four hour plane ride away? What if she was in the hospital dying and I did not make it back? What if she fell and broke something?

The same could be said of the hospital stays. When one of the parents was in the hospital, I still had the other parent. That made it easier to enforce the "we are not staying up here all day" rule. Both needed their rest and I did too!

Most often, we would visit for 2 to 3 hours, go home to rest, and then go back for a few hours. When it was just Mom, if siblings were in town, we took turns. If not, I would keep the same schedule as with Dad since she was accustomed to it. Sometimes, we needed to be there during meals to help them eat.

While in the hospital, they were being overseen but if I, the caregiver, also got exhausted, there would be a strong chance I would get sick or need hospital care as well. I always felt guilty that I might miss the doctors.

One nasty little story as an example. Mom had some kind of an episode. We were never quite sure what to call them. Her blood pressure would drop dangerously and she would zone out, completely unresponsive. It was August and the H1N1 virus was rampant in our area.

There were no hospital beds so she could not be admitted. I kept her contained in her emergency room as other sick patients wandered the halls, in and out of the rooms. Her blood pressure had returned to normal.

Common sense said I should take her home that the virus would kill her long before her episodes, but the hospital stated I would be taking her against medical advice. I should have taken her home. She did not get sick. I did, from being in the emergency room with her.

My vacation was scheduled two days later and I dangerously drove to my timeshare beach condo anyway. I adamantly needed the break. I remember passing two hospitals on the way, thinking each time, that I should probably stop. I most definitely should not have been driving.

It was a very unwise decision. It clearly revealed that I was both emotionally exhausted and perilously sick with H1N1 - high fever, chills, exhaustion (though I could not tell if it was any different than normal), major headache, sore throat from coughing, and a few other symptoms that made me stop often. It was the longest time it has taken to drive to the beach from North Central Texas. I slept for two days when I arrived.

There are a number of triggers for feeling guilty during the caregiving process. One parent may cry about a decision. Or cry because you are leaving after visiting. Or cry because they do not like the residence home. Or cry because they are still among the living. Or just cry and they do not know why.

That happens. All of those are emotional responses to deep felt frustrations and fear of the unknown. Those fears are not ours to own or to assume as guilt. That is where having a healthy set of boundaries, previously discussed, come in handy.

In The End

Do not accept blame for the way your elderly one's life has turned out if and when they need to move to a care facility. Hold them and hug them as you would a child. Remind them of all the great things they have experienced in life, especially in their current residence.

Remind them that this is just a new aspect of their journey. It may not be what they wanted but it is real and needs to happen. Be matter of fact and put aside any guilt you may feel.

No one really wants to move out of their comfortable home they have known for years, into a care facility of any kind. It may become a reality.

We can help them accept the challenge by confronting it as the logical choice, void of any guilty emotion, that moving to a place where there are no ongoing home maintenance issues and no stumble factors, is the best option.

"A word of caution. If an adult is really negative about going to fun theme park, it can ruin a child's experience."

It is the same with the elderly. Be positive, not accepting blame or guilt for the move. It is just a natural response to their growing care needs. Soothe them when they are crying, as you would a child. Then talk about a new part of their journey, with a sense of excitement for them.

It worked with Mom. Whenever she would question the unknown of the future, I would say, "I don't have a clue, Mom. But we will figure it out together, one step at a time."

In the end, she did not require nursing care, but that would have been okay. I knew what she wanted. In the end, she got the type of hospice care she wanted. She had already made that decision known, for which I am very grateful.

The pendulum quit swinging the day she died. I had no regrets.
Did I still resent what I had given up? Honestly, yes, to some degree.

BUT, I gained much more than I gave up. I am still seeing that gain today.

I gained great memories with my parents that I would not trade for anything. Just like child birth, I tend to remember the good now, not the guilt or resentment.

Life did not turn out as I planned. In many ways, it turned out better.

Chapter Nine
Humor: Intentional Joy

Elderly caregiving does provide for innumerable comical moments.

In order to remain sane, in order to keep your heart intact, in order to be somewhat balanced, you must cultivate and grow your sense of humor.

Caregiving is tough and intense. If you know me, you know I love to laugh. That came from my parents and our often shared laughter.

Sometimes in caregiving, it feels there is nothing to laugh about. There are plenty of those days. On those days, step aside from caregiving and go have dinner with friends. Ask them to tell you the funniest thing that happened that week. You must laugh.

My family learned to not be afraid to laugh, even in the intense times. It took some training and discipline but we did our best.

Like the time Mom fell off the second step of the stool while reaching for a glass casserole dish off the top cabinet shelf. She knew I was upset that she was up on the step stool, as I was looking at her much swollen elbow, which was later discovered to be cracked.

With a shimmer of mischievousness in her eyes, she exclaimed, "LOOK! I did NOT break the dish!" We laughed all the way to the emergency room.

Sometimes, Dad would stand behind Mom when she would be upset about something and make faces. Because we would all start laughing, Mom would whirl around and he would innocently roll his eyes to the ceiling, while he was still laughing.

We laughed at what we thought we heard versus what was actually said, what they wanted in their obituaries, the doctor's glasses, a cat antic, a baseball play – just about anything was fair game for laughter.

There were "Momisms" – phrases or words that Mom would say that were funny or endearing. Such as, after dinner, soon after her last bite, she notoriously would state, "Don't we need a little something sweet to eat now?" Pretty much every night. Routinely.

Translation? She wanted ice cream. When she was in hospice, all the nurses commented on how beautiful her 97 year old skin was. I told them it was a secret recipe.

Then, with a twinkle in my eye, as they leaned closer to hear the secret, I told them it was a nightly routine. She cleansed her face every night with Clinique™ and used their moisturizer, without fail. The milky smooth look to her face was due to all the ice cream she ate nightly!

One night, Dad, Mom, my nephew and I were sitting around the table. We had challenged Mom and Dad to write their own obituaries. Mom read hers with all her accolades uninterrupted. But when she read, "Lifetime Member of the PTA," my nephew interrupted, and said very seriously,

"No, Nana, you can't put that in your obituary."

"But, I am a Lifetime Member of the PTA. That should be in there."

To which my nephew replied, "Ok, Nana. But for your obituary, you have to change it to 'recently expired Lifetime Membership of the PTA'."

I thought both my parents were going to fall off their chairs laughing. That joke lasted weeks. We believed in laughter around the table, regardless of how hard life got.

Not long after, I went on a short camping trip. Calling home to check on them, I heard tornado sirens blaring in the background.

"Mom. Are you in a tornado warning?"

"Yes." [An obvious pause because she knew they were not doing what they should be doing.]

"Are you taking shelter in the bathroom?"

"No honey. I can't get your father out of his chair to go to the bathroom."

"Give him the phone, Mom."

"Dad. If you die in the tornado, I'm going to add a paragraph to your obituary."

"Huh. What do you think you are going to add?"

"Oh, I can add it all right. You'll be gone and won't be able to stop me. I'm going to add 'too dang stupid to take shelter during a storm so he died in his chair. No casket will be used for his burial. We will just bury him in his chair since he didn't want to leave it.'"

"You would, wouldn't you?"

We laughed a long time after about that weekend.

They prepaid their funeral expenses. What a blessing that was in the midst of grief. My sister and I went with them to help them make their arrangements and pick out their caskets. Several times, the funeral home staff would slowly walk by and check on us because we were laughing loudly.

I guess laughter is truly not often heard in the funeral home. Or maybe it is hard for my family to quietly laugh.

I had told the funeral director what I wanted in a casket. I had recently seen silk screened caskets on television that looked like an old fashioned brown paper covered box ready to be mailed, with twine that had a red stamp on the end that said, "Return to Sender." But my modification was a motion sensor that played an Elvis' song when they came to view the body!

We did not shy away from conversations about death. We know that eventually we will all die. It is a part of life - why not embrace it and have fun?

Shortly after I moved back to care for my parents, my mom informed me she did not like my laugh, that it was too boisterous. I have had that laugh all my life and she has never liked it. A childhood friend used to call me machine gun because of my laugh.

Seriously? At least I liked to laugh. Often. And loudly.

For the next week after her comment, I laughed like a Hollywood socialite - tilting my head back, hand in the air, with a quietly subdued, "oh, ho ho ho – that is so funny," in a high pitched voice.

The first time I did it, I thought my dad would have another heart attack from laughing. My mom, however, was not very amused or good humored at my sarcastic response to her comment.

I kept this up the rest of the week until she finally said I sounded ridiculous, to please stop laughing that way. She conceded to like my original laugh, that it was me and to not change.

One night, I called Mom to ask her to cook a vegetable. I knew we were having meatloaf but had not decided on a vegetable, giving her the priority to choose what she and Dad wanted. I came home to find Spaghetti O's ready to go on the stove.

"Mom. You do know that Spaghetti O's is not a vegetable, right?"

She replied trying to look innocent, "Oh? I thought it sounded good with meatloaf," then quickly added, "it's what your father and I wanted."

I learned that whenever Mom wanted something, she would put the inclusive "your father and I" as part of her explanation of what she was doing. I always ended up laughing. It most certainly was not worth fighting over or getting upset about.

And yes, we had Spaghetti O's for a vegetable that night. I figured they had lived long enough to choose what they wanted.

Another time, Mom and my niece were cooking spaghetti one night together. Mom asked if she thought the spaghetti was done or not. My niece replied that she did not know but she had heard that if you threw it up against a wall and it stuck, then it was done.

My mom walked over to the utensil drawer, got a fork, picked up a spaghetti strand from the boiling water and threw up against the window.

"I hope the windows are good enough because we don't have a wall close by."

Their shared laughter at her spontaneity lasted for years, long after Mom was gone and created a warm memory for my niece, who still tells that story.

The spaghetti stuck, by the way.

When there is nothing to laugh about, I do not laugh. If it is funny, the whole room will know I think it is funny. I have been told my laughter is contagious. I have been told they knew I was in a packed ballroom because they could hear me laughing.

What a compliment to be known by your laughter. I have said it before. Caregiving is brutal. **Be known for your joy and your laughter.**

Cultivate your laughing. It can truly be contagious. Choose your friends wisely and make sure they like to laugh as well. Life is too short to be serious all the time!

In caring for the aging, there is often not much to laugh about. **Do not let any aspect of caregiving rob you of your joy.**

My dad was always the instigator of household laughter. He pulled harmless pranks on all of us kids. I am not sure that my youngest brother would agree the beheaded rattlesnake propped up in the trash can was harmless. I sure thought it was funny and I was only 5 years old.

We worked quite a few jigsaw puzzles together. Mom was notorious for stealing one of the pieces so she could be the last one to put the last puzzle piece in. When we would get close, I would go check her hiding places. One time, she sheepishly held up a sad looking puzzle piece that had gone through the wash safely hidden in her pants pocket.

After she passed away, I found at least five puzzle pieces to unknown puzzles, that she had hidden then forgotten where she put them.

Mom had macular degeneration that slowly deteriorated her eyesight. We did everything we could to create light around her recliner so that she could continue to read. We even put a floodlight up to shine over her shoulder onto a book or newspaper.

She had an outpatient surgery for one of her eyes to increase her vision. The next day, on the follow up appointment, she fell off the curb getting into the car. We loaded her up into the car and drove her downstairs to the emergency room. She had cracked her ankle.

So, now she had a patch on one eye, was bruised on the other side of her face and had a soft cast on her foot. The ophthalmologist told her she needed to keep her head down for her eye to heal. The orthopedic doctor told her she needed to keep her foot elevated for her bone to heal.

Every minute, I would have to state a mantra, "Head down, foot up, Mom!" It became routine we could not say it without laughing. That was a trying week but we sure laughed a lot!

Our sense of humor was joy that we wore freely. We chose to have joy even in the midst of some of the most difficult hospital stays.

Mom used to call the men I was interested in who she said "I let get away" as "the husbands I trained." When she was in hospice, unresponsive, three of them came to visit. I leaned in to whisper in her ear, "Hey Mom, the men I trained are here for a visit," and she made a guttural sound from her throat, that I am pretty sure would have been an audible laugh in a different time.

Humor staves away anxiety. It is a form of coping. It is good for our physical well-being. It relieves stress. It makes you a fun person to be around.

Have you heard the joke about the "Cat's on the roof?" My brother used to say that was how he was going to tell me if something happened to one of our parents.

> "A man left his cat with his brother while he went on vacation for a week. When he came back, he called his brother to see when he could pick the cat up. The brother hesitated, then said, 'I'm so sorry, but while you were away, the cat died.'
>
> The man was very upset and yelled, 'You know, you could have broken the news to me better than that. When I called today, you could have said he was on the roof and wouldn't come down. Then when I called

the next day, you could have said that he had fallen off and the vet was working on patching him up. Then when I called the third day, you could have said he had passed away.'

The brother thought about it and apologized.

'So how's Mom?' asked the man.

'She's on the roof and won't come down.'"

Our household laughter thankfully never stopped. Maybe you did not come from a house of laughter. It is never too late cultivate it.

Mom loved sending and receiving emails but she always forgot her passwords. During one of my speaking engagements, when I talked about the necessity of secure passwords, an attendee told me he always forgot his password so "Iforget" became his password.

I decided that would be a great password for Mom. Surely, she could remember "Iforgot" as her password, right?

I received a distress call one afternoon.

"Honey, I know you changed my password to one I would remember but I can't remember what you changed it to. Can you tell me?

"Iforgot," I replied through my laughter.

"Seriously, honey? You can't remember it either? What good is the password if even you can't remember my password?"

After I stopped laughing, which I actually have not even now, I had to explain that "Iforgot" was indeed her password.

We laughed through the next week on that "Momism."

Laughter is not just relief or healing for you but your elderly loved ones need to laugh as well. Growing old can be frightening to them and laughter can lighten that anxiety. If their existence is always a serious demeanor, it takes a toll on their health. It is also okay to be silly with them.

One boring afternoon, I was using up some film and decided we would do a silly photo shoot in the living room. I had them get different hats and different sets of clothes. I used a wide angle lens and a tripod. I took one continuous shot, simply covering the lens between their change of clothes and hats. They positioned themselves in various places in the living room, carrying on conversations with themselves and each other in different clothes and hats, all in the same room. It was hysterical and they had fun with it.

We were silly. For the life of me, I have no idea where those pictures are hidden away. The memory of them still brings joy to my heart and was such a fun afternoon for all of us.

Sometimes you laugh when you really want to cry. During those times, it is amazing how much better I felt when I laughed instead of cried. Do not get me wrong, crying was also cleansing but laughter is the best medicine of all.

Dad needed surgery to place a stint in his renal artery. The cardiologist whom we had gotten to know well, assured him it was going to be an easy surgery - "a piece of cake" were his exact words. It was to be an in and out day surgery but he might have to stay one night just to make sure he was okay.

After the promised piece-of-cake-45-minute-surgery fell into its third hour, I became a bit nervous. I was not getting any information from the hospital staff and no one had updated us. I was later informed the stent was lost in the renal artery and they had to go "fetch" it. He was three days in ICU and another week in the hospital itself.

It was a tense scary time. Needing to lighten the moment for me and everyone else, I went by the Staples™ office supply store and bought one of their red buttons for Dad to have in his hospital room. Every time the cardiologist walked in, Dad would press the button and he and the button would proclaim together, "That was easy!"

We all would start laughing, probably only because Dad was okay at that point.

Laughter is infectious and on many of the hospital visits, regardless of how critical a parent may be, the doctors and nurses would join in our laughter, as odd as it may have been.

Two weeks before I turned 40 years old, I was preparing for a big backyard birthday bash by clearing limbs from a recent storm. It was the first time Dad let me use the chain saw, while Mom was arguing with him about that wisdom. My argument was that he needed to teach me how to us it. He would not be able use the chainsaw for many more years. After cutting up some of the debris, he was satisfied I knew what I was doing and went with Mom to pull weeds from their garden.

Later, while seated in the backseat of the car with a towel wrapped around bleeding fingers, I listened to Mom fret over the potential loss of my fingers and the endless "I told you so's."   I was trying to not get any blood on their cloth seats while Dad drove us to the emergency room. Dad smirked, looked in the rear view mirror at me and said, "I have a question."

"You moved home to help us, right?" Pause. "Who's helping who now?"

I got absolutely no sympathy as he told everyone in the emergency room, doctors, nurses and other patients, that I had moved home to take care of them in their elderly years. Thirty-three stitches later, he was still laughing all the way home.

Finding joy in life is a choice, with laughter being a result of contentment and happiness. Humor needs to be your strongest matter of the heart when caring for your elderly one because laughter is a necessary sanity tool to make it through with great memories!

Remember, sometimes laughter starts by simply smiling.

Chapter Ten
Faith: Concrete Belief System

I struggled with including a chapter on faith, because I did not want this book to be only for Christians. Regardless of what religion you are, or are not, you will find yourself clinging to what you believe during your caregiving years.

Faith believes in something beyond yourself, in a God bigger than you. Faith seems not to be a popular topic these days. Everyone has a worldview of some kind, a belief system in something, even if it is in no one. A belief there is no God is a belief nonetheless.

The focus of this book is to encourage you in the matters of your heart as a caregiver. I would be completely remiss if I did not address faith. Many of you will come from a variety of religions, a variety of belief systems. Your caregiving is often driven by your faith and/or your religion.

Of one thing I am fairly certain, most religions teach to respect and love the elderly. Hindus, Muslims, Buddhists, Jews, and Christians all have the belief that we should respect and care for the elderly.

As a Christian, I clung to my relationship with the Lord during those caregiving years. The responsibility of caregiving was not entered into lightly but with a great amount of prayer. When I prayed about whether to move home to take care of my parents, the answer was firm and sure, beyond any doubt. Caregiving is not an aspect of life to be entered into without firm guidance.

Every second of time with my elderly ones needed a great amount of trust, a great amount of prayer, and a great amount of perseverance.

Trust has never come easy for me. As a Christian, I learned that the Lord was faithful to be there beside me in my life. He has been the only constant in my life, actually. Family has moved away or moved back, friends have come and gone, but the Lord has been through all of my life with me, good and bad.

Having a concrete belief system was acquired by learning and studying. I have been blessed with many biblical, theological and philosophical learning opportunities. I took part in Bible Study Fellowship™ for seven years, some of those years during my caregiving role. I read countless books, studying and analyzing and thinking through many of my faith's complex questions.

It was not in the studying that I saw the Lord's presence most in my life. It was in how I felt cared for while I was caregiving day to day. It was as if He had asked me to do something that He knew would be challenging, He knew would be a heartache, that He knew would test my resources and He wanted me to know that He was there beside me every step of the way.

When I started my business, I trusted Him with my calendar, scheduling clients. I still do. When clients would call and cancel their appointments, I knew He was rearranging the schedule for something that needed to be done. It happened many, many times. He cleared my calendar when Mom had a stroke and was in hospice for nine days. He cleared my calendar this week as a dear friend passed away. He completely cleared my calendar to finish this book. I am just as sure when it is at print that my calendar will fill back up again.

When funds would get low, I would get a speaking engagement, a new client or more books would be sold. I have never truly advertised my business or any services or books. I was always afraid I would have more work than I could handle with the caregiving responsibilities.

There was a foundation of trust built over my life. Because I had sought answers regarding the wisdom of moving back to caregiving, I knew I would continue to be provided answers during those caregiving years. The Lord had been tried and proven in my life many times.

Faith Community

My mom and dad attended their church for over fifty years. They were active members, participating in various areas and activities. They belonged to the same Sunday School class all those years. Mom sang in the choir. Dad was a greeter and an usher during the offering.

They had a community of people with similar beliefs and they grew old together. They had picnics, spaghetti suppers, and ice cream socials over those fifty years, and they were there for each other as some in their class lost their spouses or children. They did life together.

It was important they stay connected to that community, so we did what was necessary to encourage it. My nephew, parents and I went to three different churches, even when they could no longer drive. According to the church service schedules, either my nephew or I would drop them off and the other one would pick them up. Sometimes I just went with them because I loved seeing everyone in their Sunday School class.

We prayed together as a family. We had interesting theological discussions. It was always interesting to hear their perspective after living through many events in their lives.

We even discussed heaven, whether we would truly know one another, would it matter and what size mansions we wanted. Their elderly years are not the time to question nor abandon their faith. It is the time to support it.

My nephew lived in a back room of the house not far from my parent's bedroom. He said the one thing he misses hearing is them praying together at night after they had gone to bed.

Both Mom and Dad passed away as we were singing hymns. When we sing a hymn now, if I shut my eyes, I can still hear my Dad's strong voice belting through as it did sitting beside him in church many years ago. "When we all get to heaven, what a day of rejoicing that will be!"

Anthems were most often a declaration of faith through whatever trial or period of life the writer had encountered. My parent's Sunday School class could raise the roof with their heartfelt, tried and proven, testimonial voices. There are only a few of those voices remaining here today.

They were good people, with great hearts. Their children are like my cousins. We were a family, brought together by our faith, sealed by life itself.

Having a deep running faith can also have a profound effect on your elderly loved one.

Our faith guides ethical decisions. Being involved in a faith based community held me accountable and provided love, compassion, much prayer support, and many meals.

My church community visited when one of my parents was in the hospital, they ran errands, took Mom somewhere, and were just generally available to do whatever was needed. They were available to help but I was not always good to ask for help or be specific about what I needed.

Faith Is A Personal Choice

During the Atlanta tornado in 2008, it had been a year that weekend since Dad had died. I had spoken at a dental convention a half day the day before, all day that day and was to speak the next morning. I had just returned to the top floor corner hotel room from a fun dinner out with my host and a friend.

I had recently been studying King Jehoshaphat in the Old Testament. He had quite a life, but I loved his testimony through the many different trials in his life, even through his mistakes.

> *Alarmed that several armies had joined forces against him, he stood with the men, women and children in front of the temple courtyard and prayed the most beautiful prayer that ended humbly with, "For we have no power to face this vast army that is attacking us. We do not know what to do but our eyes are upon you." They stood there waiting.*

> *Then, the Spirit of the Lord came upon someone standing in the assembly. "...Do not be afraid or discouraged because of this vast army. For the battle is not yours, but God's." "You will not have to fight this battle. Take up your positions; stand firm and see the deliverance the Lord will give you. O Judah and Jerusalem. Do not be afraid; do not be discouraged. Go out to face them tomorrow and the Lord will be with you."*

My friend that joined us for dinner had just started caregiving for her dad. I shared with her a few truths I gained from Jehoshaphat's life.

- Admitting you do not have a clue as to what to do is actually freeing. No one knows what to do 100% of the time.

- When faced with a seemingly impossible situation, prayer is always better than panicking.

- Have others stand with you in prayer until you know your answer. This does not always mean physically as I had my prayer warriors on speed dial.

- The battle is not ours. I was simply a soldier in caregiving. I only had to take my position and stand firm. The Lord would take care of the rest.

The conversation of trust and the Lord's provision would be tested not an hour later as a tornado ripped through my hotel room. I locked myself in the bathroom, as if the lock was going to keep the tornado from coming in. The noise was intensely loud. If it sounded like a train, it was a freight train, running hot and heavy, and running over/through me.

The hotel room was physically moving from the tornado's intensity, the water sloshing out of the toilet. I had tried to leave but the suction was powerfully strong. I could not open the front door. I grabbed my tennis shoes out of the closet and put them on, put my cell phone in my pocket so they could identify my body, and began praying out loud something like this:

"Well Lord, I thought we were headed down a different road, but it is all good. Please take care of Mom - I know this will kill her. Take care of my goddaughters, Lord. They will not understand and you will have to help them. Please give my brother and nephew patience to help Mom. And everyone else is on their own. Thanks for an awesome life. I get to see Dad sooner than I thought!"

I had to yell to hear myself pray, the tornado was exceptionally loud. It lasted longer I suppose because I was at the widest part of the tornado on the fifteenth floor and not at the bottom narrowest. My body felt like it was being physically pulled apart, but I felt at peace.

After the tornado and we had made our way down the flights of stairs, we were evacuated to the basement as there were other tornadoes on the radar.

Someone I met there suggested I had lost my faith because I was shaking. Just the opposite, I knew why I was still alive, especially after I surveyed the fallen roof and the blown out glass all throughout my room.

The misunderstood shaking was the physical response to a severe barometric pressure change within my body.

I have been in tornadoes, severe storms, and earthquakes with my faith still intact. Caregiving for 16 years was still more intense and more difficult than all those combined.

Faith can waver but it should not be shattered. Faith is a matter of trust. Some say it is a blind trust. Basically, I believe my God is big enough for all my needs. I have witnessed His provision for me time and time again in my life. It is definitely not a blind trust. Why would I suddenly decide not to trust during a major trial or heartache? To me, faith is similar to an athlete's muscle memory. It is remembered by my heart.

During my caregiving years, a friend committed suicide. Our community was stunned because we had no forewarning. One of the many things my faith has taught me is if you are in a tough time, just wait. Something will eventually change. It will not stay tough forever. Time is often the best aid for perspective. Suicide is not the answer.

When I would become overwhelmed, I would remember scripture long planted in my heart. I knew then the reason for all the Bible Study, so my heart could reference it when needed.

One was from Colossians 3:2:

> "Therefore, since you have been raised with Christ, strive for the things above, where Christ is seated at the right hand of God. Set your minds on things above, not on earthly things."

During those moments, I would remember that the chaos created here on earth is temporary, that though it felt it would last forever, it would not.

Another verse was from Psalms 46:10. After losing a dear friend suddenly, I was looking for scriptures she may have underlined in her Bible. I found one. This was it. "Be still and know I am God." That scripture felt like a direct message to my broken heart. I have clung to that since during heart breaking times. When I had no clue what to do, I learned to be still.

You may question God's mercy as you watch your loved ones deteriorate through aging. It is okay to question but this is not the time to throw out your own faith. You will experience a myriad of emotions. Whatever your belief system, realize everything will be called into question: God, afterlife, angels, demons, whether we will know one another - everything.

If you find yourself in a depression, please seek counseling. If you belong to a faith community, seek prayer. Faith requires trusting in what is not often seen and we need the support of a faith based community to help us through life.

In 2005, when we discovered Mom had colon cancer, we had a tough decision to make – whether or not to have surgery to remove the cancer. We met with many cardiologists, she went through many tests and there was great concern because of her normally elevated blood pressure.

Here is an excerpt from what I wrote during that time:

> I have a hope - it is anchored in Christ. If everything else in my life moves, leaves and is never heard from again, He is still beside me until I am with Him fully. Just as my life becomes richer, so does my faith because the Lord has proven Himself to me over and over again. I've had many things assail me in life, many losses. Time and time again, the Lord has been faithful to my heart, walking with me every step of the way, sometimes no more than a toe at a time.

> I don't "hope" in things that change or waver. I plan and think ahead the best I can. But I fully understand that in the blink of an eye, everything could and can change – things and relationships. I get it and have lived through it.

> Joshua 1:9 is quoted often with emphasis in different areas. "Have I not commanded you? Be strong and courageous. Do not be afraid; do not be discouraged, for the Lord your God will be with you wherever you go."

*My life's focus has been on the "wherever". What a promise – God will be with me **wherever** I go. Period. No ifs, ands, or buts. There is no circumstance that He would not be with me. He will be with me **wherever** I go."*

It was the "wherever" in this verse that Mom clung to before, during, and after her surgery. We acknowledged our faith and trust together through prayer as a family. We included the doctors and the nurses. Surgery was a big decision and they warned us many times that she might not live through the surgery. Mom lived another six years after that surgery!

During another tough hospital stay for Dad, I decided to print out my favorite verses on long strips of paper, put them in a vase and read one when I would go to visit. It was good for all of us to be encouraged.

Your belief on what happens after we die will also affect your caregiving. You may be asked about what you think. If you are asked about what you think by your elderly one, please be wise in your response. It may not be the time to expound with all the philosophical views regarding the subject of death and afterlife. If an elderly loved one is asking, they are basically asking for some consolation or reassurance, knowing they are facing imminent death, sooner than later. They may be asking for peace and permission to die.

Dad often could not attend church and Mom would not go without him. They would watch the Methodist Church they attended first on television, then they would watch the Baptist Church down the street. Dad was raised Baptist and he enjoyed listening to their music and sermon.

One Sunday, Dad and Mom seemed agitated after watching one of the church's sermons. They said the pastor had stated that we would not know each other in heaven, that it was a myth. Dad was pretty worked up about it.

That sermon led into several hours of conversation about our beliefs on death and heaven. My first response was that the Bible did not say we will not know each other, it just does not say that we do. I agreed that we will not have bodies as we know and we laughed at what size and height we wanted for our new bodies.

They wanted assurance that we would know our loved ones in heaven, as they were approaching that time. It was a little late in their life to suddenly change what they had held dear all their ninety plus years. And Dad said he was looking forward to seeing his mother again, after losing her when he was only 13 years old.

After a very lengthy discussion, I finally asked, "When I call you, how do you know it is me?" Dad looked at me and said, "Because I know your voice." "Don't you think it will be the same way in heaven? We may have new bodies but I bet we recognize each other's hearts and voices and spirits through our love for each other." It was the only way to reconcile what he had heard in the sermon and to give him peace.

Listen during those conversations. Do not dismiss their concerns. Your elderly loved ones are the ones that are imminently facing death, not you. Listen to their heart, their fears and do not correct what you believe is wrong in their theology.

Remember, caregiving is not about you. Simply love them by listening to them and figure out a way they can finish life with peace.

I wrote often as a cathartic release for whatever I was feeling. Here is a poem of sorts during a trying time in 2005:

Sustenance and strength Lord.
Surprise me with Your love.

Overwhelm me with Your joy.
Lift me up and enclose me in Your mighty arms.
Hold me to Your chest.
I want to hear Your heart in this.
I need to rest there.
Help me to rest there.

It's 3 a.m. again.
The night is quiet except for the pinball inside my head.
I forgot to call Dad's cardiologist.
I forgot to call Mom's eye doctor.
Should he be on hospice yet?
Slowly, very slowly, they are leaving this earth.
It's the rollercoaster of eleven years of caregiving.

I asked her if life had turned out like she had planned.
She smiled and slowly shook her head.
The cancer had taken all but her last breath.
"No, dear," was her warm reply
With glistening eyes.
"But the Lord has been faithful throughout
every breath He has given."

Every breath of life is a gift. Life is His gift.

Chapter Eleven
Protection: Love Running Deep

My love grew deeper for my parents through the sixteen years of caregiving. The three of us had not truly been close when I grew up. They were fully entrenched in their lives when I came along in their 42nd and 43rd year of life – surprise! At best, we learned to put up with each other. Through those years of caregiving, the many aspects of my parents that I did appreciate and love in them blossomed.

My dad was very involved in politics. He was actually a simple man, with a deep intellect, insight and analytical mind. He was a home builder in his younger years and remodeled homes in his later years. His business model changed as he grew older. I think he was just tired of falling off roofs.

I thought his favorite meal was navy beans and cornbread throughout my childhood. I did not realize those were the times he did not have a client, a house to work on, or the weather was interfering with his building schedule.

Mom made a game of shopping out of the bent-can or label-less can basket at back of the grocery store. "I don't have the right spices for dog food so try not to choose that can."

My dad was a hard worker and provided for his family. Though he was not one of the wealthiest in the community, he was still one of the most involved in the community. And, his wisdom commanded respect. I shared him with the city of Arlington, the Arlington Independent School District and First United Methodist for the first seventeen years of my life, but I had him to myself for the last thirteen years of his life.

We spent quite a bit of time just talking and a lot of laughing. My dad and I had a special bond – we thought alike, so our conversations covered many topics. Mom was always a little jealous of our relationship. It was not very surprising that after Dad passed, Mom's defensive barriers were gone and our relationship grew.

Make no mistake. It was not easy. It was a choice.

That choice was less difficult because of an existing foundation of forgiveness. On that foundation, love could be built and would grow.

As that love grew, so did my radar of protection. I became the mother hen over Mom.

One day while shopping in the local mall, we wandered into a bookstore. She had heard of a book that she wanted to ask if they had. I wandered off a little ways to look at something that caught my eye when overheard the clerk with a disgusted voice reprimand my confused elderly mother with, "We will not carry that book in this Christian bookstore."

I quickly walked over saying, "Come on, Mom," and we walked out of the store. As soon as we exited, I asked her what book she wanted. It was a controversial book written about a near death experience.

I was infuriated and Momma Bear came out in me with all claws.

Sitting my flustered Mom down on a bench outside to rest, I returned to the store and asked for the manager. The clerk tried to leave after the manager returned but I asked him to stay, recounting what had happened.

I asked him if he had a mom and what would he do if his mom were elderly and someone had just treated her that way. Would he be as mad as I was because he should be?

The store manager was only slightly sympathetic. I guess he figured Mom should have known that book would not be sold there either. His apologies certainly felt insincere and I never shopped at that store again as a result of how my elderly mom was treated.

I had to laugh at how protective I had become of my mom, though.

The elderly are very childlike in nature. Dementia can make them even more childlike and vulnerable. There are the unscrupulous who try to take advantage of their vulnerability and naivety.

If your elderly one is still living independently, make sure they understand that there are those who will call on the phone saying the most frightening things.

If the caller wants any personal information or bank or credit card information, tell them not to give it to the caller regardless of how convincing they may seem.

The greater degree of dementia equals less ability to understand, retain the information and its warnings. You might need to take away credit cards or use the parental controls for the internet. In extreme measures, their computer may need to not have internet access.

There are phone scams that target the elderly. Not the IRS, nor police department, nor sheriff wants anyone's bank account or credit card information. If they had a warrant out for their arrest, they would just show up at the door, not call ahead of time. Microsoft will not ever call about anyone's computer having a virus.

I just returned from jury duty today where the jury bailiff warned of a new phone scheme targeting the elderly population. The caller tells the person there is a warrant out for their arrest because they did not respond to a jury summons. The caller conveniently does not take personal credit cards for the "fine" but the fine can be paid with a prepaid debit card that can be purchased at any store.

The caller bullies the phone answerer into fear that if they do not follow through, law enforcement officers will arrive on their doorstep within minutes to arrest them in front of all their neighbors and friends. This scheme is extremely fear based and an elderly one's self-protection against fear wains with age.

Please inform your elderly one that they could potentially receive a phone call that would ask for payment. Regardless of what they are told, they are to hang up and call you. Regardless. Then you should notify law enforcement.

No government agency should ever call you and request payment over the telephone. If you think it is valid, always call the telephone number you have for that agency, not the telephone number they may give you during their phone call. Always be very wary of any phone calls asking for payment over the telephone.

Mom received an email supposedly from our internet service provider. Thankfully, I had just walked in the back door before she clicked For More Information. It stated she needed to "upgrade" her service and she was about to get her credit card to enter the information to upgrade. I walked in just in time.

Getting Mom to not open the door whenever the doorbell rang was impossible. She had grown up during a time one always opened the door. She would dismiss my concern every time. "Nothing's ever going to happen from me opening the door!"

They also grew up during a time everyone could be trusted. Every now and then she would read something outrageous on the internet. I often explained that just because it was on the internet, it did not make it true.

Parental controls became available as Mom's days were coming to a close. If your elderly one is on the internet, it would be a good idea to check out those controls for their computers and tablets and phones. Make sure they also have a good antivirus and malware protection system, kept up to date automatically and automatically protects. They will click innocently on everything that pops up.

Sadly, there is an abundance of fraud targeted towards senior citizens that the FBI has a webpage dedicated to the information and prevention.[1] I was actually surprised at the schemes the FBI listed as concerns regarding the elderly:

- Health Care Fraud

- Counterfeit Prescription Drugs

- Funeral and Cemetery Fraud

- Fraudulent Anti-Aging Drugs

- Telemarketing Fraud

- Internet Fraud

- Investments Schemes

- Reverse Mortgage Schemes

I would add Home Repair and Maintenance Scams. I live in a storm prone area that, when after a storm, is barraged with telemarketers selling me a variety of repairman's services. All they need is a credit card for the deposit.

Make sure all your elderly one's telephone numbers are listed on the no call list (**https://www.donotcall.gov/.**) The telemarketers will still call regardless of the number of times told the phone number Is listed on the no call list. The telemarketer's telephone numbers can be reported but their numbers most often rotate to not be the same number calling every time.

When any of my three elderly ones were in the hospital, I knew which doctors were to see them. After Chris was in the hospital, I received the Medicare Summary of which doctors had charged Medicare and there was a name I most certainly did not recognize. I found out he was not a specialist when I called his practice asking for the information regarding his consultation. After many phone calls without answers given, I called Medicare to let them know that doctor had not seen Chris, that it was a fraudulent claim. I also called the hospital to inform them of the fraudulent Medicare claim since he had hospital privileges.

It did not affect what Chris had to pay but in the long run, fraudulent Medicare claims will affect the money available for generations to come. It is also health care fraud, prosecutable and highly unethical. I talked to Chris about the doctor and she did not know who he was either.

If your elderly one is in the hospital and you cannot be there, check in with the nurse's station to inquire what doctors had seen your patient. Keep a list if you are in a hospital of many hospital doctors. They all bill separately.

I would encourage you to go over potential frauds and scams with your elderly one. Start a conversation. Talk about the types of people that do these things, that they look normal, not often what they would think a criminal would look like. Do not try to cover the whole list at once. Revisit the topic often, asking if they had received any strange phone calls lately.

A facet of my business includes examining and compiling evidence when an employee steals from a professional practice (dental, medical, veterinary or chiropractic.) My mom was always fascinated with my embezzlement cases. I was expected to report about whatever case I was working on during dinner.

She found them as exciting as reading a murder mystery. I used that time to talk about the embezzler and how the doctor always trusted them as an employee. But, it was still hard for her to translate that information to what could happen to her because not everyone could be trusted.

Most often, elderly do not report the crime. They are embarrassed. Those who got away with the crime, live on to perpetrate it with another victim. MetLife™ published a study on Elder Financial Abuse, June 2011.[2] "The annual financial loss by victims of elder financial abuse is estimated to be at least $2.9 billion dollars, a 12% increase from the $2.6 billion estimated in 2008."

51% of the fraud was conducted by strangers, 34% by family, friends and neighbors, 12% by businesses, and 4% Medicare and Medicaid fraud.

While Medicare and Medicaid fraud happen less frequently, it cost the most. Medicare and Medicaid fraud cost the victims $38,263,136. Business fraud cost $6,219,496. Family, friends and neighbors cost $145,768. Fraud by strangers cost $95,156.

Women were victims more often than men.

How do you protect the innocent when you cannot be with them 24/7?

- Make them aware. Talk about what bad people are doing these days. Keep the conversation ongoing.

- If they live independently, make sure their home is secure. Are the locks working effectively? Is there an alarm system the elderly one knows how to use? Do the windows still lock?

- Oversee their finances to ensure appropriate donations.

- Place an alert with the credit card companies to phone you personally with every attempted transaction.

- Review their credit card charges on their monthly statement or online.

Always engage them in conversation about what they did that day. You may be surprised at what they tell you.

My neighborhood now belongs to NextDoor™, a neighborhood forum. If there are door to door scammers, or stalkers for empty homes, in the neighborhood, they actively call the police as well as put it on NextDoor™ for others to be aware. I called the police on one the other day, offering to trim my trees. He did not have a truck or any equipment.

If your elderly one is still living at home, their neighbors are hopefully keeping a watchful eye on those who go door to door. It is sad that there are those in our society who will take advantage of the elderly in such a way.

Making them aware will help protect them. And give you peace of mind.

Chapter Twelve
Turmoil: Family Strife

Parents and siblings can learn miscommunication better than anyone around us. They know exactly which buttons to push, at exactly the worst time. They can jump to conclusions and judgments way quicker than anyone else around. They can perceive a tone of voice based from prior history, when none was intended.

I have heard many stories about conflicts in the families during and after caring for a loved one. It is common. It is stressful. It is often a real battle, with real casualties.

The conflict often begins with a sense of entitlement: wanting something of value to better their own lives or just because they believe they deserve whatever it is they want.

Inheritance. If you look up the meaning of the word "inheritance," you will not find "the reason many families split up after a parent has passed away," though it should be included.

When my maternal grandmother came to live with us in 1979, we built a one room efficiency guest house attached to my dad's already existing workshop. Grandmom agreed to pay for the materials and we supplied all the labor. By "we," I mean all of us. My dad, brother, niece, and I worked every day on the little house, framing, hanging sheetrock, painting, etc. My mom took my grandmom to pick out paint, curtains, carpet and fixtures.

When she died a year after the house was finished, I witnessed my uncle berate my mom, demanding half the value the little house brought to the property. He was in real estate and kept throwing out numbers. It stopped when my dad intervened with the facts of the arrangement and the costs my grandmom did not cover.

The damage was done already with Mom's relationship with her brother. Greed got in the way of his relationship with his own sister. It would have destroyed their relationship but Mom told me many years later, that she could just imagine how her mom would have felt, had she let it.

Pleasantries were exchanged and Mom was cordial because, ultimately, she loved her brother. He was the only one remaining in her family and eventually, their relationship healed, not because he apologized or was remorseful. **She did not wait for him to be sorry as she forgave him first.**

Mom never confronted her brother, which modeled to me any potential situations in our own family. The earlier you communicate with your siblings and other family members effectively, openly and honestly, the better chance you have to avoid conflict later after your elderly one has passed. That whole conflict could have been avoided had they shared with him in the first place the arrangement Grandmom had made with my parents, costs included.

How to handle those types of conflicts had been modeled by my parents during my life. It was the "don't rock the boat" philosophy. Apparently, in our family communication boat, everyone sits really still so no one falls overboard in anger or mistrust. We never challenged inappropriate behavior unless it was the parent to the child.

My oldest brother ended up caring for Chris for the last six months of her life, from another state over 6 hours away. He called once to complain about everything he had to do long distance, but then said, "I guess that's why we do it because of the inheritance."

No. That is not why we do it. If it is, then you should not be caregiving.

He never took her to a doctor's appointment. Never had to do her laundry. Never had to take her somewhere she wanted to go. Never did her yard work. Never cleaned her house. Never had to wait for doctors at the hospital. And, when she died, I made all the arrangements before leaving for a speaking engagement out of state. I planned the funeral I could not attend. I went through all her remaining belongings he had helpfully moved to a storage unit, first taking what he wanted, leaving me the bills.

Her cardiologist's nurse and he were the last ones standing and inherited the money. It reminded me of the cakewalks done at a fair when I was a kid. Chris's music had stopped and they won the "cake." They both spent very little of real life with her but they inherited the tangible. And I had no regrets in my caring for her - that was invaluable.

It did provide an opportunity for conflict. My oldest brother, Chris's power of attorney #4, decided he was going to take the cardiologist's nurse, power of attorney #3, to court for her portion of the inheritance, primarily because she had already spent the money obtained from the sale of Chris's house and she received part of the life insurance policy. His attorney called me for more information.

At the end of that very interesting phone call, the attorney asked why I was not suing them both, that I would most certainly win. Mom was still alive. To sue her son would have broken her heart and over what? Money? He was still my brother. In the end, that is the way Chris left it. It was her decision.

Greed somehow always creeps in with a strong sense of entitlement. Every time I was angered about the inheritance and the time I spent, I felt guilty for feeling selfish and greedy.

Years can be wasted in emotionally charged family arguments. During conversations about care for family members, some family members may be tempted to bring their own past, current and future hurts and arguments to the table. That is not the time.

I have one friend who does not speak to their sibling because of harsh words over how the parents should be cared for in their later years. Listening to my friend, it would appear the parents did not even have a say over what would happen to them. They were left out as the siblings fought.

Another friend has filed a civil suit on behalf of the parents' estate of which they were executor because one of the siblings, who lived on the property owned by the parents, stole from the parents' bank accounts and homestead prior to the remaining parent passing. The parents' wishes in the wills could not be fulfilled due to the sibling stealing. If they did not sue their sister, she would be not held accountable for what she had done.

It would seem that our parents' aging becomes the straw that breaks the camel's back, the ignition for an already existing time bomb. An opportunity for extremely bad behavior. A life of bitter rivalry does not change overnight. It certainly did not happen overnight.

Another friend's last parent died. The parent had told one adult child their end of life wishes, then told the other adult child something very different. Nothing was documented as to what their last wishes were and the conflict separated the two siblings because they both believed what the parent stated to them individually was what was truly desired. The parent actually caused the argument after they had passed away.

A dentist told me that the son of a deceased father requested the dentist go to the funeral home to remove the father's gold teeth. The son stated the will did not include the parent's teeth and he thought he would monetize the opportunity. The dentist declined.

Story after story of siblings no longer speaking after the parents have passed is heart breaking. It is sadly too often a reality. Chances are the family did not communicate well in life and the end of the parent's life was the emotional deal breaker. And, quite frankly, some siblings sadly do not have a sense of right or wrong.

There is a reason many books have been written on how to communicate. It is a valid topic. It is a difficult topic. A family of adult siblings is the most difficult point to start learning how to deal with family conflict. If there is an ongoing family conflict, it sabotages an atmosphere in which to build trust to be vulnerable with each other.

During a conflict, most of us have a fight, flight or freeze response to feeling threatened. We may stand our ground, regardless of how impractical or illogical the argument. Or we may retreat, taking our ball home, threatening to never return. Or we do nothing, because we are stuck and cannot move on. None of these options help foster the relationships you need, in order to best support your loved one.

We tend to feel more judgment or criticism by our family members. We love them but we may not like them or their choices in life. We may feel disrespected and unheard. We may choose friends who like and accept us because we do not get that opportunity with our family.

I reached out to a few friends who have had conflicts with their siblings to add to my list of suggestions on how to handle family conflicts in caring for their parents. Here are our suggestions on how to circumvent conflict:

- Do not take for granted the primary caregiver. If you do not live close, call often and offer encouraging words. Help them to know how much you appreciate their sacrifice. Back up your words with gifts of appreciation, such as flowers, gift cards, movie theater tickets, etc.. While you are able to freely live your life, the caregiver is not.

- Meet and agree to hire help that your parents need. If they are still living at home, this includes lawn care and house cleaning. But, make sure this does not place a hardship on their financial resources. If it does, divvy up the amounts between the siblings. Start a separate bank account each of the siblings can contribute to monthly to help defray any needed costs.

- Everyone will have their own opinion as to what the parents need and when they need it. Some will differ as to how the parent is actually doing. Have the parent(s) tell their children how they are doing during a family meeting so the children can ask questions and all hear the same answers.

- In the midst of caregiving, make sure everyone knows their specific roles and descriptions, so that everyone knows each other's responsibilities as well. There are less chances of not meeting expectations, just as in a job.

- If you are overwhelmed with caregiving responsibilities, do not assume your siblings will know. Reach out to them and see if they can relieve you for a week off. It is okay to give up control if that control is overwhelming.

- Be approachable. If you are the sibling that is always confrontational and angry, you are not approachable by anyone in the family. In that same regard, speak less and listen more. It cannot be that important to always be right.

- Listen to each other without interrupting. My family has the gift of interruption. We are a family of attention deficit siblings. We will interrupt the most serious of conversations to point out the squirrel climbing up the tree outside. However, it is a means to disengage from the conversation. Focus on what is being said.

- When we interrupt, we give the impression that we do not care about what the other person is saying. Not interrupting is a discipline that needs to be practiced more often.

- Listen without formulating your powerful response. Just listen. Listen to the other person's heart. Ask questions about what they said to clarify what they mean, without accusation or demeaning language.

- Focus on the issue at hand, not the past. Leave emotion out of the conversation. This is really hard to do if it is an emotional moment, such as losing a parent. There is always something to be decided. Focus on what that is at that moment, using the "I" statement approach, not blaming or pointing the finger at the other person.

- Do not share your sibling anger with your children. Wanting your children to take your side is emotionally immature. If they take your side, only hearing your chosen details, of their own accord, as an adult child, that is their prerogative. Choose to not be a negative influence.

- Walking away from a conflict and storming out of a conflict are two different responses. Remain calm. Sometimes perspective is needed that cannot be gained at an intense moment of conflict. It is okay to excuse yourself calmly to take some time and take a few breaths.

- A great way to avoid conflicts is to document in detail all the parent's wishes so there is no confusion as to what the parent wants. Have the parent preplan their funeral with the local funeral home. They can choose their casket and their headstones, as well as begin to pay on those options. Many arguments begin over what to choose after the parent is deceased.

- Realize there are things you cannot fix and people who do not think they need to be fixed. There is no relationship that can be controlled. Others will respond how they want to respond regardless of what you want. You cannot legislate how other people feel. That means you agree to disagree. Appreciate their uniqueness.

- If a conflict arises at the hospital regarding the care or concern of your parent, most hospitals have a social worker on staff available to help you. If they cannot help, they can provide direction to an available resource.

- Make sure parents have shared all the details of what their wishes are when they die, as well as the will, in a family meeting with all siblings present, prior to any crisis, so that all can be discussed candidly. Then document those wishes in a living will.

- Speak honestly and openly about what lies ahead in caring for a parent, including death. Understand that everyone may handle it differently, or some not at all. Do not be afraid to bring up the topic before it is too late.

- Do not be afraid to seek counseling or a mediator in a family conflict. Even healthy families need assistance occasionally.

- Do not let an elderly one's choice as to how the inheritance is divided cause havoc to your relationship with your siblings. The death of a parent is a very emotional time. Do not say what you will regret later.

Remember my reference to Big Fish, Little Fish in Chapter Four? It truly applies throughout the book, perhaps more so in dealing with family strife. Not every argument, every battle needs to be a big battle or it will tear whatever family you have apart. In fact, most of those battles are probably little battles. Choose your "fish" wisely.

In the end, you only have one family. Agree to disagree and move on.

Chapter Thirteen
Grief: Letting Go When It's Time

Mom had such a great and full beautiful week in March 2011. She had played bridge twice, gone to church for a luncheon, beat me in a game of cribbage, and had lunch with my brother. I remember watching her from my windows in the guest house, in the back yard, waiting for a ride to come by, the day of a luncheon at her church. She was standing in the sun with her casserole dish, smiling and happy.

She was 97. I was very proud of her and loved her so much in that moment for making the best of her life.

My brother and she signed a DNR (Do Not Resuscitate) document from the doctor's office that Thursday afternoon. I made copies of it, putting one in my purse and one in hers. I was just about to put another copy on the side of the refrigerator and decided I needed to make sure she knew what it meant. "Yes, of course I know what it means."

"No, Mom. You tell me. What does this document mean?"

She put her sassy 97 year old look on and said, "It means, LET ME GO!"

Little did I know that at 9:30 the very next morning, I would be handing that document over to the EMTs to take to the hospital. She had a stroke at the table writing cards to send. She was stiffly stretched in her chair, as if she was fighting the stroke. One of the firemen made a sarcastic comment about whether she was just sleeping, because she was making a snoring sound.

As loved ones were gathering in the emergency room, my brother and I were insisting on going back to be with her. It increased to a demand as they were taking long to assess her condition. My concern was her existing dementia making her more combative with increased confusion - out of her normal environment.

When the chaplain came to the emergency room, someone finally listened that I was the primary caregiver and that Mom had dementia. He made the call and took us both back.

It was as I suspected. Mom was fighting them to take her blood pressure. As soon as she heard my voice, she stopped. She could not speak nor open her eyes but she heard my voice. I rubbed her feet while they took her blood pressure. She could still move one leg and stroked my arms with her leg, letting me know she knew who I was.

At one point, the doctors left the room, I moved in to whisper in her ear, letting her know I was there with her, that they would run some tests, but this may be the day she had been waiting for, to go see Daddy.

The doctors returned and were concerned that her heart rate was dropping before they were able to do a CAT scan to assess the stroke's damage. They wanted to give her medicine to increase her falling heart rate. I kept saying she had a DNR but the doctor was persistent.

When he left, a nurse quietly asked, "What would your Mom want?" I confess. I knew what Mom would want but my brother and I gave the okay for her to have the medicine. It was the one decision I regretted. It is hard to make decisions in the moment, especially when the medical information is incomplete, and when truly I was the one not ready to let her go.

How do you make the decision when you do not know the damage?

In hindsight, that is exactly why Mom and I had that conversation the day before. I knew what she wanted but that was the only conversation we had about it. She was ready to go. I just did not understand how much she was ready.

When they moved her to ICU, her primary care physician arrived with another doctor he wanted to assess Mom. The CAT scan did not show a hemorrhagic stroke, which shows immediate bleeding. It was definitely a stroke but they did not know to what degree.

I was already feeling guilty about giving her the meds to increase her heart rate. I knew what she wanted and at that point, it had already been four hours.

She still was not opening her eyes, nor speaking, and had stopped moving. I felt she could still hear but I told that doctor that Mom had made that decision for us by signing the DNR.

We made the decision to move her to hospice downstairs in the hospital. It had been converted from the nursery where my niece had been born forty years prior. I was thankful my youngest brother was there to help make that hard decision. By mid-evening, she was resting comfortably in hospice.

In hospice, they no longer continue life sustaining medicines. They will provide food and water if the patient can eat on their own. They will provide morphine as needed for comfort. They will keep them clean with baths (bed), clean sheets and clean gowns. They will keep their mouths clean.

Let the hospice staff do their job. If you have questions, ask them. I always had questions and they were always nice to answer them.

Most hospices have snacks available or they know which restaurants will deliver. Dad was in a standalone facility that had ample sitting nooks, outdoor walking paths and a small movie theater supplied with popcorn and movies.

Mom's hospice was connected to the hospital. It had a snack room, with a freezer full of ice cream and popsicles. It seems like I really enjoyed the snacks but when you are in an unknown situation it is helpful to have food available so that it is not necessary to leave hospice.

The nursing staff in both facilities was exceptional and their care and respect of my parents in their last days was comforting. Hospice staff truly minister to the hearts of the dying and the living.

Saying Goodbye

In hospice, the patient needs to hear they have permission to die from all the family members. Some may linger simply because they believe they need to stay for whatever reason.

When Dad was in hospice, the nurse asked if there was an anniversary or birthday that he could be waiting for or if all the family was there yet. My oldest brother was unable to come but I was not sure that Dad had heard that news.

It was nice that there was no one in his room. I could talk to him openly and freely without upsetting anyone. I leaned in close to him to make sure he could hear me. I recounted what the nurse had asked me and that I was wondering if he was waiting for my brother to arrive.

I told Dad that my oldest brother was unable to make the trip at this time, that he had to choose now or a funeral because of work, and that he wanted to be at the funeral to support Mom. I told him it was okay to go ahead and leave, that his body was done. I told him we would take care of Mom and not to worry. I told him that I loved him and what a great Dad he had been. Dad was completely unresponsive. I had no idea whether he had heard me or not. I held his hand and kissed his cheek.

Everyone came back within just a few minutes. We read a few special emails I had received out loud, then we started singing. It was Palm Sunday so we sang a few of their favorite hymns. Daddy passed away about 25 minutes after I told him it was okay to die. We were singing "How Great Thou Art" when his heart beat for the last time on the line "and when you come to lead me home." He was ready to be led home.

The timing was not lost on me. I understood he was waiting. The nurse told me that those that are very close to their families will wait until they have all arrived before dying. It is the dying one's way of saying goodbye.

She also said that introverts tend to die when their room is quiet and their loved ones have left. Extroverts wait until the room is full. Both of my parents waited until everyone was there and the stage was set!

Nine days was a long time in hospice for Mom - someone who could not eat or drink or speak or move. We used those nine days to talk, recounting fun memories, telling funny stories she could no longer deny because she could not respond. And there was lots of laughter.

The nurses in Mom's hospice asked me the same questions - was she waiting for someone. No, we were all there and waiting with her. I had given her permission, as did my siblings the best they could. I honestly believe she was cognizant enough that she just did not want to miss anyone who would come to visit.

I truly felt horrible for her - she was trapped in the shell of her body. She was unable to speak, move or open her eyes until she passed away. I do know she could hear because she would purr in my ear when I would get close to speak to her.

And she growled when the doctor visited. That was really funny. The noise was a definite guttural low toned growl. It startled the doctor but we were laughing. Astonished, he said he had never been growled at before. I knew her well enough to explain to the doctor to not take offense. I believe she growled because she was ready to go and did not want to be fixed.

While proofing this book, my niece shared she had told Mom that her son or daughter would be waiting for Mom when she arrived in heaven. She had not told her grandmother she had lost their first baby. Mom groaned when she was told.

Because hearing is the last function to truly go, you should always talk as if they can hear you. We played her favorite music, we read aloud, we had conversations as if Mom was a participant. It was a revolving door of friends and family coming to visit us and to say goodbye to Mom. She tried to move when my niece from out of town arrived and she squeezed the hand of her best friend, my godmother.

The nurses reiterated many times that it was my time to not be the caregiver, that my job was done. It was time to be the daughter once again, for her remaining days. A few friends came up during those long days and took me out to dinner. That was nice because I needed a break.

Early one Sunday morning at 4am, the ninth day, I awakened suddenly, and knew I needed to get dressed and go to her room. I had an hour and a half with her to myself, reading the Bible, holding her hand and talking to her about our lives together. I talked to her about seeing Daddy again, asked for another trip to the World Series for the Texas Rangers™ and some other personal heart to heart loving. It was a sweet time.

An hour and a half later, my brother and his wife came with the same story. They had awakened suddenly and knew they were to come. I gave them their time to be with Mom.

An hour and a half later, my sister and brother in law arrived with the same story. We all left the room so they could have their time with Mom. It was as if Mom was gathering all her chicks to say goodbye.

My oldest brother had to return to his work and was unable to be there. He had that time with her before he left, knowing it would be his last.

The hospice nurses had shared with us the stages of death that we could physically look for:

- Cannot open eyes or speak
- Fluctuating body temperature - the brain can no longer effectively regulate body temperature and is in the process of shutting down
- Irregular or shallow breathing
- Low bladder output
- Weak pulse
- Low blood pressure
- Skin color changes starting with the feet

We all gathered again in her room that morning as the nurses came to do their rounds. They said they felt it would be soon and left. We talked a while but then started singing hymns, like we did with Daddy.

I noticed Mom "looking" different and stood up to be beside her. We started singing one of her favorite hymns, "I Come To The Garden Alone," which she used to sing with my youngest brother who was holding her other hand. I could tell she was leaving. I leaned in to whisper one last permission. I had promised to walk her to the gates of heaven but then I asked her to let go and keep going towards her loved ones there.

The last breaths of life can be intense. Some have reported a death rattle sound. Both Mom and Dad just gulped for air and were gone.

I was surprised at the silence that filled the room immediately after each of them passed. Maybe that was me feeling the emptiness of their loss. There is definitely a wave of varying emotions after losing a loved one.

When Dad died, I felt the intensity of grief but I did not allow myself to be overwhelmed by the emotion because I still had to care for Mom. I had to be strong for her. Immediately after Dad died, I was helping her to bed to take a nap. She said she did not think she could live without Dad. I lay beside her, wrapped my arms around her and said, "You have to. I'm sorry, that's not an option." We both laughed. "Mom," I said quietly, "I can't lose both of you in the same year." "Yes honey, I know. I'll try."

Three years later with Mom, I was intimately involved in funeral plans again. My caregiving services were no longer needed as of March 20, 2011. It was a little weird. Much of my life was spent caring for them that there was an immediate void. The to-do list was long and I avoided the grief I knew would be overwhelming. I still had to attend to all the details of the funeral and the estate.

Dad and Mom purchased their funeral home arrangement plans with a friend of theirs who worked at a local funeral home. After Dad's funeral, that friend retired and a friend of Mom's had a bad experience with that funeral home. Mom asked me if she should move her arrangements to a longtime friend of our family who had opened a local family owned funeral home. He was also very dear to my mom's heart, as his grandmother lived across the street when we were kids. It was easy to transfer her prepaid arrangements to other funeral home.

After Mom passed away, I was thankful that Mom had transferred her arrangements to be at my friend's funeral home. I trusted him to care for my mom, even in death, as he tenderly cared for me as well.

Since we had spent a good deal of time talking about what they wanted at their funerals, some of that planning was already decided. We had the celebration the way they wanted it. In fact, for Dad we had a private burial in the morning, with the memorial service in the afternoon. This helped give Mom a much needed break. Mom liked it so much that she requested the same sequence of events for her funeral.

After the visitations for each of them, before the casket was sealed, the family gathered in front. We put special things from us to be buried with them in their caskets.

With Dad, my youngest brother that shared a love of fishing with him put a lure in his pocket. My sister who had an ongoing joke with him about Tube Rose snuff every Christmas, put in the two cans that he was to receive the following Christmas. One grandson put in a Louis L'Amour paperback book because Dad loved his westerns. I added a single rose I had cut that day because we loved to garden together. And the famous pancake spatula used by Dad every Saturday morning for family breakfast was also included.

With Mom, it seems there was more sentiment. One granddaughter put in the recipe for the cinnamon rolls that she made every holiday and they had begun making together a few years before. Mom's best friend put in two Goo Goo bars because Mom loved them. We all put her Texas Ranger™ baseball cap on her because when she wore the cap, they won games. My brother put a cribbage board with a deck of cards for all the games we shared.

Years before, she had worn a pair of pink cotton pants with an elastic band around the waist. She decided the band was too tight, so she cut down a seam in the back, which showed her white cotton underwear every time she wore a short waist shirt. She wore them all the time and out often in public.

I threatened one day in frustration that I would bury those pants with her because she loved them so much. I did.

Putting all those "love mementos" in her casket gave us another means to say goodbye. It gave us another great memory to share.

Since Mom loved ice cream, we had an ice cream social in the fellowship hall of their church after the funeral. My nephew had bought a large variety of ice cream bars, cones and sandwiches. Everyone commented on how that was so Mom!

Your elderly one's "home going" funeral celebration should:

- Be the way your elderly one wanted, regardless of how zany and unusual

- Honor them

- Celebrate a well lived life, regardless of the age

- Focus on the positives

- Create opportunities to laugh and cry at the same time

- Be led by someone who actually knew your loved one

- Listen to all the great stories from their friends that you will hear from others and keep them in your heart

One friend's dad was cremated and did not want a funeral so there was no funeral. Funerals are not for the dead but to give the living an opportunity to say goodbye, a time for mourning. If there is no funeral, there could still be a graveside service or a family gathering to recount stories.

I have also heard the nightmare stories of how the parents made no pre-funeral arrangements at all, nor made their wishes known. The ones responsible then just had to guess.

If there were no directions left by your elderly one, use wisdom in making those choices. Here are a few things to consider:

- Would they have wanted cremation or burial? Cremation is less expensive but this may have some conflicts with their religion. Be sure to check and be respectful.

- If they chose to be cremated, in many states they must sign cremation documents. If these are not signed, the family can go against the parent's wishes in cremation.

- Set a budget. It is expensive. Do not let the emotions of loss sway you to spend more than you can afford for funeral costs.

- Was your elderly one a veteran? There are funeral benefits for veterans. Consider burial in the national cemetery. And in the local cemetery, the designation of their branch of service is free for the headstone, as well as a flag folding and presentation ceremony from their military branch of service.

- If you are only making arrangements for one elderly loved one, and still have a remaining spouse, consider only paying for one burial plot at this time, and pay for the other plot monthly. Since they are often on a strict monthly budget, this will help with their out of pocket expenses.

- If the elderly one had a life insurance policy, for a small processing fee, you can assign the benefits to the funeral home for the funeral costs and another assignment for the cemetery costs. They are both only allowed the amount designated on the contract. This may vary depending upon what the state regulations allow. You will need the insurance company name, policy number and a contact.

I have heard of funerals that were led by pastors or priests that had no relationship with the deceased. These funerals are most often talked about as being cold and impersonal. If the church must have their pastor in charge, I suggest that the family also appoint someone who knows the deceased to do the eulogy.

Just as in caregiving itself, everyone's experiences in death and celebration of life will be unique. Pay attention to your heart. Your grief will be a culmination of all you have felt for however long you have been caregiving or longer.

The truth is Dad and Mom may have been 94 and 97, but it was still too soon for me. I miss them every day and am very grateful for the gift of memories.

Chapter Fourteen
Resolve: Life Moves On

The funerals are over. The caregiving has drawn to a close. Nothing was left but the paperwork and the closing of the estate. Life slowly moves on.

The day after Mom's funeral, I sat at my parent's round kitchen table with four others talking. The whole house smelled like a flower shop, with flowers and plants in every room. It was overpowering.

Mom had the year before put at least fifteen vases in a box that she was going to give away. I knew we had at least two times that many in the garage cabinets. So, we all jumped into action.

Two washed and dried all the vases. Grabbing the large aluminum serving pans that once held dinners brought over, three started taking apart all the large sprays. Flowers and ferns went in to separate pans. One had taken a flower arranging course and helped the rest arrange some beautiful, much smaller arrangements.

Then over the course of the next few days, we delivered the flowers to friends of my parents, taking the time to visit with them. Several of them were unable to physically come to the funeral so that visit was very special for them. All of them told endearing stories about one or both of my parents.

Special for them. Healing for us.

There were mounds of thank you notes to be written for the food, flowers and special items. There would be many more to be written in the future as well. When Dad died, we established a scholarship fund at their church. When Mom died, we asked that contributions be made to the scholarship fund as well.

We divided up the list and wrote the notes at their kitchen table. The notes to specific friends of the siblings were given to that sibling to write the thank you notes.

When you are the power of attorney and the person is no longer living, you have no authority. The Executor is now the one that begins the process of settling the estate. At the time that my parents made their wills, no one lived in town but me, so I was both power of attorney and executor.

I found insurance policies that they had from long ago that we did not know about. The bank accounts were already in my name as well as Mom's. Paying the final medical, funeral, and normal bills was then not hard. The attorney did his thing in sending the appropriate paperwork to the siblings to settle the estate.

It took months to take care of everyone but I know that is still a relatively short time compared to some estates. There were mounds of mail and documents that needed to be completed. Death certificates go quickly as it seems all entities need an original, not a copy, of the death certificate.

I had a box I put all the mail and documents in so nothing would be lost in the chaos. If I was overwhelmed that day, I would just throw the mail in the box and wait until I was no longer overwhelmed. I realized that could not be forever as some documents were time sensitive.

The sibling's inability to communicate as a group, as a family, however, caused hurt feelings that could and should have been avoided. It still would have been hard. We had all just lost our last parent.

Words were said in anger that never should have been. Accusations were said that are difficult to forget. I would say we were a pretty normal family when I listen to how all other friend's families made it after their parents' funerals.

In the end, what our parents wanted was fulfilled.

I had always prayed my parents would die in their sleep, mercifully. Neither one of them did but selfishly we also got to say goodbye. Every trip I went on, I wondered if they would be alive when I returned. They were alive, and as old as they were, I was still surprised at how their lives ended.

I had also selfishly prayed that Mom would go first since Dad and I got along well. That did not happen either and I am really glad. Mom and I had three great years together.

Some feel relief when it is all over. I think being single may have changed that for me. My parents were my family and now they were both gone. I felt very alone. Though I did have my siblings and nephews and nieces, it was still very different. They belonged to their own family group. I did not. I think that made the loss perhaps a bit more intense.

Losing my parents is not my first gig at loss by any means. It was just the most intense loss. Birthdays and anniversaries are difficult. I miss Mom making a fuss over my own birthday and making sure I had red velvet cake to celebrate. And, of course, ice cream.

I miss Dad's excitement on Christmas morning, eager to get in and open presents. I see Dad in my nephew, who gets excited about hanging the Christmas lights outside. The anniversaries of their deaths can be somber days. We try to do something that they would enjoy, even if it just means being together.

Grief can be overwhelming at the strangest times. A song comes on the radio. You see someone who reminds you of the one you have lost. Every time a picture of Queen Elizabeth is on the television, it reminds me of Mom. I always wondered if she was related to royalty.

In those moments, tears flood your eyes, there is a catch in your throat, and your shoulders sag, all typically followed by a deep sigh. Those moments are healing, as hard as it may seem. I am thankful for our ability to retain memories and as time moves on, the bad memories seem to be less for which I am thankful.

I have learned that it is okay to be a little bummed every now and then, but the loss cannot be the focus of life. If one lingers too long in grief, without moving on, it can cause a deep depression and stalemate in life, greatly affecting your future. I knew my parents would never have wanted me to be stuck in grief.

179

Grief can be overwhelming. It is different when it is your parents. Your parents have been the one stabilizing force in your life, at least mine were. Being single, their death left me without a family. The overwhelming feeling of being an "orphan" is real, though I most certainly did have the blessing of having parents.

Mom and Dad read the Upper Room Daily Devotional Guide every morning before breakfast together. After Dad passed, Mom read it by herself. I found it on the table when I returned home from the hospital the day of her stroke.

After she passed, I was straightening the house, getting ready for company before her funeral. Saturday, March 19, 2011's devotion was titled, "God Never Leaves Our Side," written by Doris Yeung from Thailand about the loneliness she anticipated when her parents would die.

She quoted John 14:18: Jesus said, "I will not leave you orphaned; I am coming to you." Though Jesus was not talking about when we lose our parents, I felt He was comforting me that day because I had been grieving the loss of both my parents. I keep that reminder on my study bookshelf now.

The Letters

A few days after the funeral, my nephew and his best friend were going through filing cabinets and items in my parent's bedroom and the "junk" room. Since it was obvious they were looking for something, I asked. My nephew replied that Mom had written all her kids letters. He said he had walked into the den one day and, when she had not heard him, he looked over her shoulder to see what she was writing.

That was news to me. I had no idea she had written anything to us. They gave up after a thorough search and I figured I would find them sooner or later. There was no designated place for important documents that she would have tucked them away in.

The next week, life had slowed down. Relatives had gone back to their lives. I had begun to wonder what to do next. I needed to start cleaning up and out the house but I was pretty tired. I decided to start where Mom spent most of her day – in her recliner.

She had an arm caddy that hung over the recliner's left arm full of items: 11 fingernail files, 15 used toothpicks, a puzzle piece, 4 pens, 2 pencils, unused (I think) tissues, 3 soda can pull tops, finger nail clippers, and a few other assorted random items.

On the coffee table between my parent's chairs were a few magazines, more pens, her Bible and Guidepost™ devotional, the remote control holder, a letter recently received, a tissue box, and a clipboard with notepaper where she documented her blood pressure readings.

I laughed and cried as I cleaned out the assortment of stuff around her chair. I remembered stories of her using toothpicks and my reprimand to stop using them. She had irritated her gums one time allegedly using toothpicks and she defensively told me that I only worked for dentists, that I was not one. I wished I had thought to bury her with those toothpicks left behind.

And I wondered how many fingernail files does one need or can one use at one time? There were enough fingernail files for each finger.

As I picked up the clipboard to see if any of her recent blood pressure readings indicated a stroke, I noticed paper on the bottom, sticking out of the right side. Pulling out the blood pressure reading papers revealed four envelopes. Four sealed envelopes, addressed to each of the four kids.

I sat quietly in the recliner for a few minutes before I opened the one that bore my name. There were three letters in my envelope. The first one I could tell she wrote shortly after Dad passed away. It had additions and revisions in the margins that she reconstructed into the second letter. The third letter I could tell she had written recently as her previously beautiful handwriting was less ordered on the unlined paper, a result of her macular degeneration.

An excerpt from the second letter, rewritten from the first, said:

"Dear daughter Susan (the Caboose) —

Thank you so much honey. You've been here and helped us when we needed you. Dad was in the hospital so much – you knew how to talk to the doctors and to get Dad the very best care. I know it wasn't easy to keep your business going while all this was going on but you've made it very successful, in spite of all of this going on. I'm so proud of you and Dad was too."

"Honey, thanks for watching over me – taking me to the library – making me (reminding me) to take my meds, making sure I eat lunch, taking me to check on my hearing aids and my glasses."

The third letter was pretty much the same, being grateful and recognizing the heartfelt love and care she experienced. It was reassuring to my heart to read that she felt that way since it was not easy for her as well. And it was certainly a warm legacy to leave behind.

But being a mom came back even after she had passed, as her third letter contained the following admonition:

"Keep trim – you have the good looks! Someone is probably out there waiting for you – needing you!"

She switched pens to write this as it was added in a darker black ink for emphasis. Through tears streaming down my face, I burst out in laughter. Mom had her last "gotcha."

The first one was signed "Love, Mom." The second was more eloquent at "My love & blessings, Mom." The third one fit the content of her letter – to the point at "Love you, Mom."

When I gave my youngest brother his letter later, he said quietly as he turned the letter over in his hands, "Mom had closure. These envelopes were all sealed. She said what she needed to say in them. And she was ready to go; a little like her bags were packed, waiting at the back door."

He was right. What a blessing that letter was to me. I reread them again to write this but have thought of them so often since she has been gone. They have been a source of encouragement to me when I needed her little kick in the pants to keep moving forward. Just seeing her handwriting brings a smile to my face.

Over the next few months, my youngest brother and I slowly sifted through all that was left behind of our parent's lives. The phrase "you can't take it with you" is true. The "junk" room had three filing cabinets full of papers and bookshelves full of books, journals, photo albums, and postcards from exciting places.

We found genealogical research documents on long gone relatives she had hunted down. We found love letters from Dad, written to and saved by Mom. We found journals Mom had written in college. She dated three guys at once – that would have been a fun conversation to have with her! We never knew about those journals, I am guessing for that reason.

We found letters of ours she had saved. We found articles from newspapers of things we had done or accomplished that we never knew she had clipped. We found pictures of those we assume are related but we are not sure who they are. One of them is a very old wood framed portrait that was put away in the very back of the closet. I think he is my maternal great-grandfather but I have no idea. I love the portrait so he is now watching over the living room.

Tucked away in some papers, I found a yellowed 4" x 6" sheet of paper with Mom's handwriting. It was perhaps notes taken from a Bible Study or maybe she was trying to write down Bible verses she remembered. We will never know but I have it framed and placed on the fireplace hearth. Her random verses are followed by something that reminds me of Mom and is very akin to my own ADD:

> "Be strong of good courage
> Thy word have I hid in my heart that I might not sin against thee
> He that watcheth over thee neither slumbers nor sleep
> The Lord is my Shepherd
> Isaiah –
> Fear not for I the Lord thy God will uphold thee
> 2nd Chronicle 14
> If my people which are called by my name
> Wait upon the Lord
> He that dwelleth
> Bring cards."

Bring cards. I laugh every time I see this on the fireplace mantle. I am not sure why she included that phrase at the end of those scriptures but, to me, it almost seemed that in the midst of the spiritual aspect of life, remember to enjoy life as well.

That, or she wanted to remember to take cards to heaven. Good thing we included a deck in her casket.

Finding treasures like this random sheet of paper are healing in grief. They are reminders of relationships in the past with parents, friends and family all waiting to be discovered. I took time to read each one and decided whether to keep it or take a picture of it and throw it away.

I made piles of things to be donated, things to be given to family, things that just needed to be thrown away, things I definitely wanted to hang on to, and things I would at some point in the future let go of but not that day. Photo albums were the hardest to decide what to do with. If they were pictures involving a sibling's family, the pictures went to that family. If the pictures were of their friends, I would keep a few of the best pictures to give to the siblings to remember them by.

We had a garage sale for big items that I would not keep, such as the kitchen table and chairs, couch, tables, lamps, etc. Clothes and most everything else was donated to her church's resale store or to the local mission outreach.

When grief would be overwhelming that day, I would stop. I did not place any unreasonable expectations on myself for accomplishing everything within a few months. It took time. There is no formula for working through grief. Just one day at a time.

If grief is overwhelming you, there are many opportunities for grief support groups in churches, hospitals, therapy groups and even retirement communities.

Moving on is healthy. It does not mean forgetting or leaving them behind. It means treasuring all the memories and taking them with you through the remainder of your life.

How has caregiving changed me?

In the midst of the most stressful caregiving days, I realized I would never be the same again. My life had become a pattern of waiting for the next crisis to happen, planning ahead for every possibility. It had been difficult to make firm plans with friends, never feeling free to take a real vacation, etc.

I wondered so many times who I was going to be when all the caregiving was over. Honestly, I was not sure. Stress had become a natural part of my life, like a built in feature. I was not sure if there would ever be such a thing as a normal life again, though I am more convinced now that there is no such thing as normal!

It has been over five years since Mom passed. I am just now starting to feel more like myself. The return to "me" started in 2015, when I turned 59, four years after the conclusion of my caregiving responsibilities. I took a long look at my health and did not like what I saw. I had gained an astronomical amount of weight and my third knee surgery resulted in my knee not being the same as it was before surgery.

I used to be active, enjoying camping, hiking and biking, among other outdoor activities but the more intense the caregiving became, the less active I became.

I used to love to read and listen to music, but the more intense the caregiving became, the more I simply wanted quietness.

I found it difficult to make personal plans for the future, and I hesitate even now as if I do not know that I can make future plans yet.

I did not want to be in the same rut as I turned 60 and I am in process of reclaiming and repurposing my life. I changed my routine and my diet.

I work out daily. I am gluten free which makes it easy to give up bread. I do not drink sodas. I drink a large amount of water. I have lost 40 pounds so far and love my newly reclaimed energy level! My knee still gives me grief but it is much stronger now. I feel much healthier.

But, I am also:

- More compassionate
- More passionate
- More aware of the elderly
- More in the moment
- More intentional

I find myself more mindful of gray headed seniors in the grocery store. Or when I open doors. And I keep a watchful eye out for them in the parking lots. I take the time to talk to them wherever I am because I am not quite sure if they have had a conversation with anyone that day. I know at some point in the future that will be me.

I am very aware of what is ahead as I get older. I want to make sure I have my affairs in order as we do not ever truly know our expiration date. I have researched and purchased long term care insurance. I work with a financial planner. I have made my wishes known and those wishes are documented.

My nephew and niece have divvied up the future (very future) caregiving responsibilities and my niece is to care for my brother and his wife and my nephew gets me! He says I will be easy, as he has already contributed to caregiving.

Those are the positives. There are some negatives, as I expected. I will continue to focus on the positives so they can choke out the negatives.

Slowly, I am learning to dream again. I can set goals again. One of my goals was to share my journey by writing this book. Many have suggested the writing of it was cathartic. Though it was fun to write about the great parts of caregiving, delving up the not so fun parts of caregiving was certainly not cathartic. It was painful but I did it to help others that are approaching caregiving with their elderly ones. Or perhaps, help those prepare to be cared for in their own elderly years.

I will never get the time back from those sixteen years, nor do I want to if it means I would lose the memories with my parents created during those sixteen years. My goal in caregiving was to have no regrets and I do not.

Loving Mom, Dad and Chris thru the remainder of their days was a blessing to me. I do believe I received much more than I ever gave. And I am grateful for the time I spent with them.

Again, it does not matter how long someone you love lives. It is never long enough. There will always be something more you would have asked. Another wise opinion you would have gained. Another laugh you would have shared. Another memory you would have created. That is the true inheritance of caregiving!

APPENDIX

Footnotes

Chapter One   Matters of The Heart

[1] Work and Family Researchers Network , www.workfamily.sas.upenn.edu

Chapter Four   Inadequacy: Role Changing

[1] TheBMJ (The BioMedical Journal), Cognitive decline can begin as early as age 45, warn experts. January 5, 2012. Archana Singh-Manoux, PhD is from INSERM's Center for Research in Epidemiology & Population Health at the Paul-Brousse Hospital in Paris.

[2] Timothy Salthouse, Department of Psychology, University of Virginia. When does age-related cognitive decline begin?   Neurobiology of Aging, April 2009, Volume 30, Issue 4, Pages 507-514.

[3] Theory of Human Motivation, Psychological Review, 1943.

Chapter Six   Heartache: Empathy vs. Martyrdom

[1] Boundaries – When to Say YES, When to Say NO, To Take Control of Your Life. Dr. Henry McCloud, September 2004.

[2] Margin: Restoring Emotional, Physical, Financial, and Time Reserves to Overloaded Lives, Revised 2014 , Richard Swenson.

Chapter Seven   Frustration: Patience Is Truly A Virtue

[1] Alzheimer's Association: "Early-Stage Caregiving, "Late-Stage Caregiving," "Middle-Stage Caregiving, "Seven Stages of Alzheimer's."

Chapter Eight   The Pendulum Swings Between Guilt & Resentment

[1] Dictionary.com

[2] https://www.medicare.gov/Pubs/pdf/02174.pdf

Chapter Eleven Protection: Love Running Deep

[1] www.fbi.gov/scams-safety/fraud/seniors

[2] https://www.metlife.com/assets/cao/mmi/publications/studies/2011/mmi-elder-...

For Further Personal Consideration

If you are approaching caregiving or are in the midst of caregiving, there are some questions you may need to ask yourself. Consider journaling, to capture your heart, as you answer the questions and, as a result, ask many more than can be answered. There may be times you need to return to read your answers, and remind yourself why you are caregiving. These questions are for you to personally consider.

Chapter One   Matters Of The Heart

- What fears or concerns do you have about being a caregiver?

- If you are not an only child, how will you make the decision on whether or not to be the primary caregiver?

- If you have made the decision to be a caregiver, how did you make that decision? What is your story?

- What is your expectation of this book? What answers do you need?

Chapter Two   Sacrifice: The Call & The Purpose

- What are your biggest obstacles in caregiving?

- Who have you consulted in your caregiving decision? Who else do you need to consult?

- Make a list of those you can consult about the wisdom of being a primary caregiver for your elderly loved ones.

- Who will be on your support team?

- What are the options to assure your elderly loved one receives the care they need today and in the future?

- What is your motive for caregiving?

- What do you need to specifically consider before becoming the primary caregiver?

- What is the maximum amount of time you have available weekly for caregiving responsibilities?

- Create a plan for the current need and future need, understanding more time will be needed later than now.

- What is the maximum amount of money you can provide towards ongoing care should it be needed?

Chapter Three   Forgiveness For Imperfection

- Forgiving does not mean forgetting. Do you harbor resentment against a sibling or grandparent or parent? This will affect your caregiving and your perseverance.

- If you are caregiving at this time, how has it affected your care? Please consider ongoing counseling during your caregiving timespan. You have a choice. There is no excuse to put on resentment and wear it daily. You are only robbing yourself and those around you of joy.

Chapter Four   Inadequacy: Role Changing

- What emotional role did your elderly one play in your life? How has that role changed in the past few years?

- What have you learned about your family history from your elderly one? Write it down.

- What tasks of your elderly loved one(s) have you already assumed?

- How are you setting the tone for how you wish to be cared for in your elderly years?

- What purpose does your elderly one have now? How can you strengthen their sense of purpose?

- How can you prepare your heart for the changes in both your roles?

- Are they eating regularly or do they need some help in preparation?

- Do they feel safe where they are living? Do you feel they are safe where they are living?

- When is the last time you did a walk through to ensure their residence is safe?

- Has anyone co-signed on their financial accounts? Bank lockbox signatures and keys?

- Are there any outstanding loans?
  Consider creating a Quicken™ accounting software file for them. It is easier to oversee all of their finances thru online access allowing you to download and update all accounts and credit cards.

- Are the beneficiaries up to date for all life insurance policies?

- Do you have a list of all the medicines they are taking?

- Do you know what the medicines are treating and how many times per day?

Chapter Five   Communication & Honesty

- Have all the necessary documents from the Family Toolbox been gathered and everyone knows where they are located?

- What struggles do you currently have communicating with your elderly one?

- What struggles do you currently have communicating with your other family members?

- How have you practiced active listening with your elderly one? And with your family members?

- How can you help coordinate a family meeting?

- What tools could you use to enhance family communication? Family Google calendar? Private family Facebook™ page? Monthly Skype™ meetings? Monthly emails?

- How can you have honest communication with your elderly one? Now is the time. Now is your opportunity.

- Please refer to more questions contained in the chapter itself.

Chapter Six   Heartache: Empathy vs. Martyrdom

- Do you feel it is wrong to have time for yourself?

- Are you being responsible or a martyr in your caregiving?

- If the answer is a martyr, what can you change to ease the caregiving role?

- Are you a martyr because your loved one is difficult to care for or because it is simply a role you have assumed? What your answer is determines what changes are needed – your role in caregiving or you.

- Do you feel guilty or afraid to say no?

- Where are your weaknesses? Where do you need to set your boundaries?

- Have you put your life on hold? Why?

Chapter Seven   Frustration: Patience Is A Virtue

- Define what frustrates you, tries your patience, in regards to your elderly one.

- How can you separate your frustration from what is the natural aging process to provide more patience in your caregiving?

- Have you noticed any signs of dementia? Does your elderly one feel they are experiencing any dementia symptoms?

- Have you talked to your elderly one regarding what their wishes are should they become mentally incapacitated? Are these wishes thoroughly documented?

- Are you clarifying the medicines for your elderly one? Are you clarifying their treatment plans?

- Have you sought out a relevant support group to help with the frustration you may incur from having an elderly one with a form of dementia, such as Alzheimer's?

- Have you verified that family members are on each doctor's forms as having permission to discuss care with the doctor or hospital?

- Have you verified that family members have permission to speak to the insurance or Medicare on your elderly one's behalf?

- Do the doctors have hospital privileges to treat your elderly one at the hospital of their choice?

- Do you feel trapped? What is a healthy outlet for you to enjoy?

- Makes a list of what makes you happy. Make a list of what makes your elderly one happy. Use these lists for ideas of things to do and enjoy, alone or together.

- Do you have a regularly scheduled FUN time with your elderly one?

- What is your end desired result?

Chapter Eight   Pendulum Swings Between Guilt & Resentment

- Do you know what your elderly one desires should the need arise for varying levels of care?

- What level of care do they need now? What potential care in the future might they need?

- Are you aware of all the possibilities available in your elderly one's local area?

- What are the viable options financially? Prepare "what-if" scenarios based on their available financial resources. For instance, how long would their financing last in nursing care?

- On a scale of one (low) to ten (high), how are you doing on the swing between guilt and resentment?

- What makes you feel the greatest guilt?

- What makes you feel the greatest amount of resentment?

- What can you logically change?

- Will you have any regrets in the care of your elderly one?

Chapter Nine   Humor: Intentional Joy

- Write down the funny stories that will happen during your caregiving with your elderly ones. You may need to recall the memory of them when things get tough.

- Are you known for having a good sense of humor?

- Ask your elderly one about the funniest thing that ever happened to them.

- Ask them to tell you the funniest thing they ever saw.

- Ask them to tell you the funniest thing they remember you or a sibling ever did.

- Ask them about the funniest movie they ever saw.

- On the tough days, practice smiling. It will help your heart and your attitude.

Chapter Ten　　　**Faith: Concrete Belief System**

- What does your religion say about how you should care for the elderly?

- What does your religion say about what happens when someone dies?

- Are there any resources through your faith's community to help you in the caregiving of your elderly one?

- In what ways has your faith deepened in the midst of caregiving?

- In what ways has your faith been challenged in the midst of caregiving?

- Have you honored your faith in your caregiving?

Chapter Eleven　　　**Protection: Love Running Deep**

- List specific areas you need to be aware of in order to best protect your loved one.

- Have you helped your elderly one become aware of those who would defraud them of their money?

- Have you ensured their computer has appropriate virus and malware protection?

- Do you occasionally review their finances to ensure there are no questionable expenses, such as out of the ordinary donations, products or services?

Chapter Twelve   Family Strife

- Be honest. How is the pulse of your family?

- You cannot control the behavior of others but you can control your behavior. What do you need to change to not cause family strife?

- What would your elderly one say about family strife resulting from caring for them?

- What decision would they have made 20 years ago, or when they were cognitively able to make this decision, to have prevented this conflict?

- Some families never see each other again after their parent's pass away. Are you willing for that to happen in your family? What can you do to counteract existing or future family strife?

Chapter Thirteen   Letting Go When It's Time

- Have the hard conversations—make sure you and your elderly one are on the same page.

- Do they want a Do Not Resuscitate order?

- Do they have a hospice preference?

- Do they want burial or cremation?

- Have they prepaid funeral expenses? Are there any remaining costs?

- Do they have a funeral home preference?

- Do they have any special requests?

- Do they want flowers or scholarships or other memorials for a specific place or designation?

- If they want, help them write their own obituary. You will then see what they considered important achievements in their life.

- Have you had a conversation about the reality of death? Have you given them permission when it comes time?

- Who will help you make decisions, in the end, should you need to?

- Have you asked specific friends to be there for you when your parents pass away?

Chapter Fourteen   Life Moves On

- Are you taking the best care of you that you can in the midst of caregiving? Are you getting enough restful sleep? Eating nutritionally? Getting appropriate exercise?

- When you finish caregiving, how will it have changed you?

- How can you honor your parent's life after they have passed away?

- What are you looking forward to recapturing in your life after caregiving?

- What are your goals for five years?

Family Tool Box

My dad was a carpenter who built and remodeled homes. The tool box sat in the back of my Dad's pickup. When he needed to rehang a door or nail a roof or tear out a wall or see if the concrete was level, he had the tool to do it in his tool box.

This is your family caregiving tool box. The documents include:

- Designing Your Long-Term Care Plan article
- Document Checklist
- Emergency Contact List
- Password List
- Personal Medical Information Worksheet
- Prescription List
- Meal Plan

All "tools" can be downloaded at:
www.mattersoftheheartcaregiving.com
Click on the Family Tool Box tab and enter the password "Iforget" to download documents.

As new tools are created or discovered that would help you in your caregiving process, I will add them to the Family Tool Box. Come back often to discover what new tools are available.

Suggested Reading

These are some of the books I read during my caregiving years. They were not about the subject of caregiving but rather the topics I encountered while caregiving.

A Grief Observed, 1961, C.S. Lewis

The Traveler's Gift, 2002, Andy Andrews

Love Is A Choice, 2003, Dr. Robert Hemfelt, Dr. Frank Minirth, Dr. Paul Meier

Understanding People, 2013, Dr. Larry Crabb

Setting Boundaries™ with Your Aging Parents, 2010, Allison Bottke

Boundaries: When To Say Yes, How to Say No, 2008, Dr. Henry Cloud

When Your World Makes No Sense, 1990, Dr. Henry Cloud

Grace That Breaks The Chains, 2014 Neil Anderson, Rich Miller, Paul Travis

Chosen for Blessing, 1992, Norman Wright, Harvest House Publishers

The Blessing, 1986, Gary Smalley & John Trent, Thomas Nelson Publishers

Margin: Restoring Emotional, Physical, Financial and Time Reserves to Overloaded Lives, 2014, Richard Swenson

Good 'n' Angry, 1983, Les Carter, Baker Book House

Good Women get Angry, 1995. Gary J. Oliver, Ph.D. and H. Norman Wright

How to Survive the Loss of a Love, 1976, Harold Bloomfield, MD; Melba Colgrove, PhD; Peter McWilliams

Understanding Grief, 1992, Allan D. Wolfelt, PhD

The Power of Encouragement, 1997, Dr. David Jeremiah

Hand Me Another Brick, 1978, Charles R. Swindoll

Three Steps Forward, Two Steps Back, 1980, Charles R. Swindoll

Online Resources

These are only a very few of the great resources available:

Agingcare.com – Connecting people caring for elderly parents
    10 Signs of Caregiver Stress
    How Caregiving Can Change Your Personality
    Six Reasons To Appreciate Your Job as a Caregiver
    If You Knew Then What You Know Now
    Family Meetings: How to Have Peace

15 Ways to Stay Sane
http://johnshore.com/2012/08/22/15-ways-to-stay-sane-caring-for-an-elderly-parent-2/

Caring for elderly parents
http://www.huffingtonpost.com/tag/caring-for-elderly-parents

Caring for Aging Parents
http://www.oprah.com/health/Caring-for-Aging-Parents-Martha-Beck-Advice

8 warning signs of health problems
http://www.mayoclinic.org/healthy-lifestyle/caregivers/in-depth/aging-parents/art-20044126

The Parent Trap
http://www.kaiserhealthnews.org/stories/2012/march/01/parent-trap.aspx

Tax help in caring for an aging parent
http://www.bankrate.com/finance/money-guides/tax-help-in-caring-for-an-aging-parent-1.aspx

Caring for eldery parents catches many unprepared
http://usatoday30.usatoday.com/money/perfi/basics/story/2012-03-25/
caring-for-an-elderly-parent-financially/53775004/1

10 Tips for Caring for Aging Parents
http://money.usnews.com/money/blogs/the-best-life/2011/07/18/10-tips-
for-caring-for-aging-parents

9 Strategies to Stop Fighting With Your Siblings Over Senior Care
http://www.aplaceformom.com/blog/7-9-14-stop-fighting-with-siblings/

Tips for long-distance caregivers
http://www.mayoclinic.org/healthy-lifestyle/caregivers/in-depth/
caregiving/art-20047057

Long-Distance Caregiving – A Family Affair
https://www.nia.nih.gov/health/publication/long-distance-caregiving-
family-affair

The Survey Says

In preparation for giving a caregiving presentation, I sent a digital survey in 2012 to over 3,500 individuals via email. The responses I received made up the following demographics:

<1%	20 to 29 years old
5%	30 to 39 years old
15.2%	40 to 49 years old
44.5%	50 to 59 years old
32.4%	60 to 69 years old
1.9%	70 years old or greater

The following are the questions asked and their enlightening answers:

What age do you consider to be elderly?

2.5%	over 60 years of age
5.7%	over 65 years of age
15.9%	over 70 years of age
23.5%	over 75 years of age
42%	over 80 years of age
10.1%	over 85 years of age

Do you anticipate caring for an elderly one?

3.1%	never
36.3%	already have done so
25.4%	now
<1%	within 6 months
15.9%	within 1 to 3 years
8.9%	within 4 to 6 years
9.5%	in over 7 years

Where are you in the sibling order?

5.7%	only child
37.5%	oldest
5.7%	next to oldest
20.3%	middle
4.4%	next to youngest
23.5%	youngest

The answer to this question surprised me. Most of my friends were the youngest child caring for their parent but psychologically, it didn't surprise me since the oldest child is typically the "in charge" sibling.

Has a family meeting been held with parents and siblings to discuss and plan for the upcoming elderly years?

33.1%	yes
63.6%	no

It is vitally important a family meeting be held, before a crisis. If there is resistance, start slow. Have a conference call with your parent(s) until they like the idea of a family meeting.

Is there a sibling officially responsible for the elderly one's care?

40.1%	yes
55.4%	no

The results of this question relate to the results of the prior question, since a family meeting had not been held to decide who is officially responsible.

Do you honestly feel equipped to care for your elderly one at this time?

48.7%	yes
35.4%	no
15.8%	no response

Total time spent monthly by all siblings with elderly ones?

26.7% less than three hours
12.1% 3 to 6 hours
8.9% 7 to 11 hours
11.4% 12 to 18 hours
24.2% 19 hours or more

Total time weekly elderly one socially interacts with others?

45% up to 8 hours
42% more than 9 hours

Remember, social interaction is vitally important for the elderly person. Even if you have to somewhat force them to go, it is good for their continued cognitive functioning. Here are a few ideas:

Schedule visits with their friends
Game /Bridge day
Have their friends over
Sr. Citizen Day Care
Church activities for seniors
Library visits

What are your elderly one's medical conditions?

39.5% Heart disease
37.9% Hearing loss
36.4% Arthritis
33.3% Alzheimer's/dementia
30.2% Depression
26.3% Incontinence
20.7% Vision Loss
17.6% Diabetes
13.8% Cancer
10.7% COPD
8.4% Stoke
7.6% Parkinson's/Tremors
Less discussed:
Depression
Anorexia – loss of appetite
Bathing – personal care

What is the one thing you wish someone would have told you before you started caring for your loved one? (Their personal responses)

- Enjoy the time, even when the duties are unpleasant. When they are gone, you would give anything for one more day, or one more conversation. Ask for help if help is available. And even if you can't get much of it, schedule some time to yourself.

- That your responsibilities are never ending, you live your life as it comes around and they are the children now. It is rewarding and demanding. Financially and other paperwork, you are questioned not just by family but by medical and state.

- That you do not have as much control as you might think. Even though the patient may be terminally ill they still have a VERY strong need to be independent and don't always agree with the limitations placed on them. They may take unnecessary risks.

- I cared for my father-in-law for the last two years of his life. I want to tell others that if you can bring your loved one into your home, by all means do it. Yes, it's difficult and there are sacrifices (expense, lack of privacy) but in the end, it is so much easier to have them at home with you than in a facility. At home, they interact with you, grandchildren and pets. You can supervise their diet and the caregiver's duties. You don't have to worry about making time to visit them, because they are already there and you spend time with them every day. We no longer have a garage (it was converted into two small bedrooms) and our guest bath is still handicap-accessible, but in the end we knew we did the right thing. I never expected to feel so good about a decision I was so reluctant to make. We are keeping the rooms and bathroom intact for when my parents need it. Everyone benefits, and you are setting a great example for your kids.

- You need to have compassion for the elderly person. Be very patient with them. They feel helpless and don't want to be a burden to their family.

- Try to put yourself in their position, pain, and be more understanding. Realize it won't last forever, and when they are gone, you will want to look back and believe you did the very best you could to make their last days on earth as easy as possible.

- Caring for our mother created a lot of conflict between my sister and me. That caused more stress for me than caring for my mother.

- If your loved one has dementia, you are not going to fix it. Just go with the flow as much as you can.

- I wish I had known and understood the impact medicines had on my parents' demeanor. There were times when I just said that is not my mother speaking to me in that manner. I wish my parents financial affairs would have been in place prior to the illness. I wish my parents had discussed what to do if this happens to us with both my sister and I.

- Yes, no way can you completely be prepared for life's changes. Your parents have always taken care of you, and suddenly, you are making decisions for them. This is a difficult transition. I think baby-boomers should be wisely informed about the upcoming changes ahead. Many are still in the workforce and have other responsibilities. Both people are working. Other siblings may live too far away to contribute, or may not want to help. In many cases, it is one adult child that does it all. I advise people to put as much energy as you can into the situation, because you do not want to look back with any regrets.

- I wish someone had told me not to make sacrifices to my own life that I would regret later. I lost track of some good friends because for three years my extra time after working was spent with Mom. I also did not spend enough time with my grandsons. My focus at work was not as good either because I was worried about Mom at home alone for part of the day. If Mom had not had dementia the situation would have been much better but we could not predict that and I had to realize I did not have the training to deal with my mother's mood swings, memory decline and depression.

- It is so very, very hard. People don't understand what we do as caregivers. No one wants to get involved. No one really wants to help out. No one offers to help us. No one comes to visit my mom - even just to say, "hi." It is so sad for the elderly - they can't do things for themselves. They feel lost at times. As someone has told me many times, "it is hell getting old...don't get old."

- It's tough, but it won't last forever.

- You are never prepared enough , the hardest part was pain control, my mom had terminal cancer and at times we do not understand "Pain". Finally spend as much time as you can with the family member . Once they are gone , you will feel you did your best and spent quality time and that is the best memory you want!

- I did not understand fully the responsibilities of the nursing home and those of the family. In retrospect, the nursing home never has enough help to do everything for the resident. I wish I had had a clearer understanding of just where their responsibilities ended and the families began. We learned by "trial and error" which can sometimes be painful.

- Caregiving can be a very lonely job, but with all of the hardships and heartaches, I would not do it any other way. I have been blessed to have this time with my mom and know I am doing the right thing for her. In our society, we are expected to "just put them somewhere." I think that is a tragic message and a sad reflection on our selfish society. Yes, it is hard caring for my mom, but I can hold my head high and know at the end of the day that I have done my best.

- I wish I would have asked more questions about their youth and growing up and recorded some of that to transcribe to written accounts of their life. I wish people would have prepared me for the gradual changes. What starts out as "doable" becomes more difficult as time goes by and conditions worsen and progress. I wish someone would have warned me that seemingly good friends will disappear and the feeling of isolation will increase as caregiving duties take over your life.

- Remember that your elder is not choosing to age with difficulties.

- It is ok to be on an emotional roller-coaster. Try not to get attached to the other residents at the nursing home. Do what your 'gut instincts' tell you to, even if you don't know why. Regular visits improve relationships w staff and thus make care better when you are not there. Take time off.

- To get more of our family history while they were here. to cherish every single minute with them, because when they're gone, you'll wish every day for one more minute, one more hug. that it's ok to take time for yourself. don't waste time being resentful towards your siblings for not doing their share, it's a waste of your energy and you need it for yourself and your parents.

- I wish I'd known that, like childbirth and rearing, the good memories would overwhelm the bad ones. The time spent together would not be regretted or resented because there is fundamental love and respect going both ways. Shared laughter is vital. Honesty and a huge willingness to be flexible when possible, and firm when necessary is critical. And never refuse help however and whenever it is offered. Allow your parent to be involved in as many decisions and actions as possible, but don't hesitate to be the final word. Your parent (especially with dementia) is child-like and it's your "parental" responsibility to keep them safe by making sometimes unpopular decisions for them. Give yourself a break.

- Don't take anything personal - remember that their world is changing and mostly out of their control which makes life very unsettling for them.

- Be patient with them and with yourself. And then be patient some more.

- Take care of yourself - seek help and support when needed (even if that help is not directly helping the elderly...maybe just helping you by being there with a listening ear)

- Pray for God's grace to extend to the elderly one!

- Caregiving gives you extra special time with someone you love--that can never be taken away. The person receiving care may not be able to say thank you, but you can see it in their eyes. Go into it, knowing that God has given you the greatest privilege.

Index

Acknowledgments

No book written is ever the sole effort of one person. That has never been truer than this book!

First, let me thank my parents and Chris for giving me so much material, though as I write that laughing, I am also serious. Had I not had the experiences I did, I would have nothing to share with you, which causes all of the experiences to be blessings. And a heavenly thanks to them for the smiles I feel in the completion of this book.

Secondly, to my family. They have endured hours of me asking questions to validate a memory, clarifying facts of things I wanted to be sure and supporting me emotionally through the process. You are my family and I love you. Thank you.

Thirdly, to all my friends and colleagues. You also endured hours of talking ideas through, what to share and what not to share, calmed my anxieties and shared a meal when I needed a break from reliving it all again. Thank you.

Fourthly, to all my amazing peer reviewers, my grammar whizzes, my editors, my friends. You questioned and sifted through all the material countless times, asked me questions, and answered my questions, all patiently. Thank you.

The process of writing a book is not easy. I am still amazed I have written so many technical books, though all of my technical books together were much easier than birthing this book. I had the "idea" of writing a book on caregiving when Dad passed away but knew I would need to wait until Mom had passed to write it. That was five years ago and it is amazing how much one person can procrastinate!

I started speaking on caregiving first and it only reinforced the need for the book to be completed. The writing process has taken over five years. In fact, the content layout was in a different direction until a wise friend coaxed the current layout into being.

I was amazed that when I needed an editor, I read about an editor a colleague had used on the National Speaker's Association™ Facebook™ page. When I needed a designer for the cover, I ran into a friend in the church lobby whose husband had just completed designing a book cover. When I needed a website built, I relied on a business associate to guide me through the process. When I needed time to just write, all business stopped. I would say it was a "coincidence" that all the pieces of the puzzle came together but it was not.

There were many days I could not write because reliving some of the events of those sixteen years wore me down all over again. There were many nights I would wake up in a panic because I was being completely vulnerable in the writing. But when there is a push from the Lord to accomplish something, I have learned it is best to be obedient.

And, here it is. The Acknowledgments page is the last page to be completed. I wanted to wait until the end to write it. Thank you. That is all – I'm DONE!

About the Author

Susan Gunn is a nationally known and sought after financial organizational expert in the healthcare industry, with a degree in Psychology, who built a successful speaking and consulting business at the same time she took care of her father, mother and step-grandmother, ultimately becoming one of the country's leading experts on healthcare fraud and embezzlement.

During the heart-warming, sometimes heart-breaking, but deeply inspirational time of her 16 years devoted to caregiving, she learned firsthand about the extraordinary power of love and faith, commitment and sacrifice, grief, joy and sheer perseverance that caregiving required. (The degree in Psychology helped, too.)

Susan combines her gift of hilarious storytelling with usable lists of concrete caregiving information and from-the-trenches guidance, combined with warm, personal, and often downright comical insights into aspects of caregiving that often go untold.

In addition to being a fiercely loyal friend to many, she has also been named 'best aunt/godmother in the world' by several nephews, nieces and godchildren who look to her for guidance regarding life experiences, humor, career expertise, down-to-earth, practical advice or just ears to listen to their heart.

A native Texan and rabid MLB Texas Rangers™ Baseball fan, she resides in Arlington, Texas with her dog, Kakie (aka "Kakie the Destroyer"), and feline pals Myrtle and Grace.

Notes

Drawing of Beth Gunn holding her great grandson by Emma Krom.

Made in the USA
San Bernardino, CA
22 January 2017